Top Skills

Advanced Comprehension

For Selective Schools and Scholarship Preparation

Therese Burgess

A
FIVE SENSES
PUBLICATION

Five Senses Education Pty Ltd
2/195 Prospect Highway
Seven Hills 2147
New South Wales
Australia

Copyright © Five Senses Education Pty Ltd 2012
First Published 2012

Burgess, Therese
Top Skills - Advanced Comprehension
ISBN 978-1-74130-751-1

Contents

Top Skills Advanced Comprehension comprises thirty-five comprehension units and four cloze exercises. The passages chosen for the units reflect a wide range of subjects and text types.

The questions range from easy to difficult within each unit and require the student to exercise a range of skills: locating specific information; drawing inferences; forming conclusions; making predictions and analysing and evaluating information. As well, the student will learn to examine the structure and language of a piece of text.

Full answers are provided, as well as tips for approaching multiple choice comprehensions and cloze exercises.

To gain maximum value from this book, the student should look back over all the wrong answers, searching the text for evidence for the correct answers. As well, they should look up the meanings of any words which are unfamiliar and write them in the pages provided at the back of the book. They can test themselves regularly, or ask someone else to test them. This type of revision is very necessary if the students wish to improve their comprehension and vocabulary skills.

How to Approach Multiple Choice Comprehensions

- Read your questions carefully. Be sure exactly what it is you are being asked. Look for key words such as 'how', 'why', 'what', 'where' and 'who'.

- Be careful of words such as 'all', 'generally' and 'always' in questions. These sweeping statements and the evidence in the text may not fit with them. For example, a question may ask, "Do lemurs **generally** approach humans?" The text may show that lemurs are very shy and only **occasionally** approach humans out of curiosity. The evidence shows that they occasionally approach humans, and so the answer is 'no'.

- If you cannot decide which one is the correct answer, proceed by process of elimination. Take away the wrong answers that you know are definitely wrong.

- Notice the title of the text. This may give clues to the answer.

- If the author of the text and from where it is taken are given, pay attention to this.

Cloze

- Read the whole cloze text through before you start. Never proceed word by word, or sentence by sentence.

- Keep looking back in the text to see that your choices fit with what has gone before.

- Keep looking onwards in the text, for clues to the word you are working on.

- Read through the whole passage when finished. Does it make sense? You may need to adjust words.

Read the extract and answer the questions that follow.

Rubber is a natural substance – the sap of certain trees. The sap is collected by making an incision, at an angle, in the tree trunk. A cup is attached below the incision and the sap drains gradually into it. Each night or in the early morning, the worker or rubber tapper removes a thin layer of bark in a downward slant. The timing is important, to avoid the higher temperatures during the day. A tree can yield latex (rubber in its pure form) for up to five years. At that time, incisions are made on the opposite side to allow the tree trunk to heal.

Rubber Plant Bengalese (Ficus Benghalensis)

In 1839, Charles Goodyear found a way to treat natural rubber with heat, sulphur and white lead. The process was called vulcanisation and meant that rubber could be utilised in many different ways; the most important being for car and bicycle tyres.

Malaysia is a big producer of rubber. It provides 20% of the world's needs and has 1.3 million hectares of land given over to rubber plantations run by thousands of small holders.

1. **The purpose of the brackets in the first paragraph is**
   a. to introduce another idea
   b. to provide a simpler word to use
   c. to give a definition of a word
   d. to show that latex has impurities

2. **A synonym for 'incision' -**
   a. amputation
   b. notch
   c. splint
   d. diagonal

3. **An antonym for 'yield' –**
   a. surrender
   b. withhold
   c. produce
   d. endure

4. **This text could form part of one of these books.**
   a. "Rubber Band Creations."
   b. "Nature's Gifts."
   c. "Tourist Guide to Malaysia."
   d. "Car Manufacturing."

5. **The text suggests that**
   a. The sap flows quickly into the cup.
   b. The rubber flows consistently at all times in the day.
   c. After five years, the tree cannot be used.
   d. The sap flows better in cooler temperatures.

6. **Vulcanisation involves using**
   a. water, heat and sulphur
   b. white lead, sulphur and heat
   c. heat, saffron and lead
   d. heat, white sulphur and lead

7. **Latex is**
   a. vulcanised rubber
   b. processed rubber
   c. crude rubber
   d. utilised rubber

8. **The importance of vulcanisation was**
   a. to increase the number of plantations producing rubber
   b. to enable artificial rubber to be produced
   c. to allow the invention of the car
   d. to expand the uses of rubber

9. **Which statement about the Malaysian rubber industry is true?**
   a. It is decreasing in importance.
   b. It has increased 20 % in recent years.
   c. It was founded by Charles Goodyear.
   d. It is based on small plantations.

10. **Which fact cannot be found in the text?**
   a. A rubber tree produces 5 grams of rubber each day.
   b. Malaysia has 1.3 million hectares of rubber plantations.
   c. The slant is cut obliquely.
   d. Vulcanisation was invented more than 170 years ago.

11. **Number these steps 1 to 6.**
   [   ] The rubber is vulcanised.
   [   ] Car tyres are made.
   [   ] The latex goes to a factory.
   [   ] The sap seeps into the cup.
   [   ] A slit is cut in the trunk.
   [   ] The worker collects the sap.

12. **The purpose of the illustration is**
   a. to explain a particular part of the text
   b. to show that rubber trees are all similar
   c. to convey information by visual means
   d. to show the size of rubber trees

13. **The information in the brackets above the illustration is included**
   a. to demonstrate the correct pronunciation of the name of the rubber tree
   b. to provide the scientific name of the tree
   c. to reveal the more common name of the tree
   d. to show that rubber trees originally had a different name

14. **Which of these statements can be inferred from the text?**
   a. The rubber industry significantly damages the environment.
   b. To benefit the environment, synthetic rubber should be developed.
   c. The rubber trees rejuvenate and thus, tapping is not a threat to the environment.
   d. The environment is enhanced by the planting of rubber trees.

15. **A phrase which has a similar meaning to 'given over' is**
   a. devoted to
   b. exploited by
   c. donated by
   d. sold cheaply

16. **'The timing is important' is an example of**
   a. an opinion
   b. a phrase
   c. technical language
   d. a statement without evidence

17. **Which of these words is not a synonym for 'utilised'?**
   a. employed
   b. marketed
   c. used
   d. applied

Read the email and answer the questions that follow

Hi Pop,

We are having the best time in Vietnam! After we arrived in Ho Chi Minh City on Sunday, we had a ride in a cyclo. This is a kind of little taxi with a seat in front and a bicycle at the back. The traffic is so busy and there are millions of motor-scooters. We saw two men carrying a big pane of glass on a motor-scooter!

We took an overnight train on Tuesday from Hue (the old capital) to Hanoi. The beds were very hard and the top bunk was so high that Mum was afraid she'd fall out in the night. (She didn't.) We saw some Water Puppets on Wednesday night. They were cool. They just seemed to be swimming about on a pond and we couldn't work out how the people working them did it. Alex said later that they were boring, but she thinks everything is boring right now. Besides, she was laughing at the funny bits.

Yesterday, we drove to Halong Bay. The rice harvest is happening now and we saw lots of rice spread out on the roadside to dry. Halong Bay was amazing. There were literally dozens of limestone islands rising straight up out of the water. We boarded a junk and travelled to a big island where there were caves with stalactites and stalagmites. It was quite hot inside the caves and we were glad to go for a swim afterwards. We spent the night on the junk.

Today, we came back to Hanoi and took a tour in a little electric bus. I'm really tired now, so I'll email you again when we get to Cambodia on Sunday.

Love, Emily

1. **Number these, 1 to 8, in the order in which Emily saw them.**
   [   ] The islands.
   [   ] The rice harvest.
   [   ] The train.
   [   ] The Water Puppets.
   [   ] The cyclo.
   [   ] The electric bus.
   [   ] The stalactites.
   [   ] The pane of glass.

2. **'There were millions of motor-scooters'. This is an example of**
   a. a simile
   b. a metaphor
   c. hyperbole
   d. personification

3. **They travelled to the caves by**
   a. bus
   b. car
   c. boat
   d. train

4. **Where did they see puppets?**
   a. Hue
   b. Halong Bay
   c. Ho Chi Minh City
   d. Hanoi

5. **What puzzled Emily?**
   a. the train trip
   b. the puppets
   c. the pane of glass
   d. the caves

6. **The caves**
   a. were made of limestone
   b. were extensive
   c. were gloomy
   d. were on the mainland

7. **Which statement is true?**
   a. It was cool in the Water Puppet theatre.
   b. Alex slept on the top bunk.
   c. Alex was amused by the Water Puppets.
   d. They had a tour by electric car in Ho Chi Minh City.

8. **Which of these facts cannot be found in the text?**
   a. The train from Hue to Hanoi travels at night.
   b. The family are visiting two countries.
   c. The train journey took twelve hours.
   d. Hue was the old capital of Vietnam.

9. **They went on the junk on**
   a. Wednesday
   b. Thursday
   c. Friday
   d. Saturday

10. **When do they leave Vietnam?**
    a. the next day
    b. in two days
    c. in three days
    d. the next week

11. **A word that means the same as 'literally' is**
    a. seemingly
    b. possibly
    c. factually
    d. figuratively

12. **Emily suggests that Alex**
    a. wanted to convey that the water puppets were too childish for her
    b. actually felt that the water puppets were silly
    c. didn't want anyone in the family to enjoy the water puppets
    d. regularly tries to spoil Emily's fun

13. **What did Emily find 'amazing'?**
    a. the caves with stalagmites and stalactites
    b. the way the water puppets seemed to swim
    c. the traffic in Ho Chi Minh City
    d. the panorama of Halong Bay

14. **Emily's attitude towards the trip is**
    a. restrained
    b. amused
    c. apathetic
    d. animated

15. **Which of these statements is false?**
    a. The train went from Hue to Hanoi.
    b. Mum was nervous on the overnight train.
    c. They took a cyclo in Hanoi.
    d. The rice is spread right beside the traffic.

16. **This text could be described as**
    a. a fantasy
    b. an almanac
    c. a saga
    d. a chronicle

Read the extract and answer the questions that follow.

The fossil vestiges of this bulky blue fish have been found in rocks dating back four hundred million years, to a period known as the Middle Devonian age. Until the middle of the 20th century, the fish was thought to have been extinct, as no specimen less than 60 million years old had been found. Then, in the 1950's, the fish was rediscovered.

The coelacanth, and its relative, the lung-fish, are the last remaining members of a group of fish that had special fins which had their own skeletons and muscles. Scientists believe that coelacanths are related to the amphibian which probably became the ancestor of all land creatures. The coelacanth has a fat-filled buoyancy organ which is like a lung, and unlike most fish, it gives birth to live young, which are called pups. The coelacanth may have been able to survive for 30 million generations by slowing down their metabolism between meals. This would save energy and stop the fish feeling hungry. It would be able to exist on a very small amount of food.

The coelacanth's habitat is the deep ocean, usually between 170 and 200 metres. The fish was able to catch prey in the deep ocean because of special abilities. It has a special flexible joint in its head, allowing its jaw to open widely. As well, a jelly-filled organ in its nose may be a device that helps in locating the electrical charges given out by prey. Divers have observed these fish doing head stands for as long as two minutes at a time, and it is thought that they might be trying to sense these charges. Coelacanths have been seen to swim backwards as well as upside down, and so these strange acrobatics may have a purpose.

Coelacanths are 'mucilaginous' which means that their scales release mucus and their bodies give out oil. The oil makes the fish inedible unless it is dried and salted. Because of this, fishermen usually throw them back!

1. **A word with the same meaning as 'vestiges' is**
   a. relatives
   b. remains
   c. bones
   d. ancestors

2. **An antonym for 'ancestor' is**
   a. relative
   b. follower
   c. forefather
   d. descendant

3. **A coelacanth would feel**
   a. dry
   b. slippery
   c. spiky
   d. warm

4. **A slow metabolism would help**
   a. to detect electrical impulses
   b. to bear live young
   c. to perform acrobatics easily
   d. to survive on little food

5. **A 'device' is**
   a. a nostril
   b. a useful thing
   c. a fin
   d. an organ

6. **The fish may swim backwards to**
   a. slow down its metabolism
   b. avoid predators in the deep ocean
   c. help it find suitable prey
   d. show its ability to do acrobatics

7. **A coelacanth is**
   a. like no other fish
   b. small and blue
   c. like a lungfish
   d. now extinct

8. **Coelacanths were rediscovered**
   a. late last century
   b. in the middle of the 20ᵗʰ century
   c. in the Indian Ocean
   d. two hundred years ago

9. **A synonym for 'flexible'**
   a. rigid
   b. elastic
   c. concealed
   d. functional

10. **Which of these sentences is false?**
   a. A coelacanth was well adapted to life in the deep ocean.
   b. Few fishermen keep the coelacanths they catch.
   c. A coelacanth lays between 170 and 200 eggs.
   d. The coelacanth was thought to have become extinct 30 million generations ago.

11. **'A special flexible joint' is an example of**
   a. scientific terminology
   b. informal language
   c. technical language
   d. figurative language

12. **Which of these sentences is true?**
   a. The fat-filled buoyancy organ helps the fish find food.
   b. The coelacanth was the ancestor of all living creatures.
   c. The coelacanth has lungs as well as gills.
   d. The coelacanth is found at least 170 metres below the surface.

13. **Which words show that scientists have not yet discovered all there is to know about this fish?**
   a. 'have observed'
   b. 'may be a device'
   c. 'these strange acrobatics'
   d. 'thought to have been extinct'

14. **Which of these words has the same meaning as 'mucilaginous'?**
   a. unpalatable
   b. salty
   c. noxious
   d. gluey

15. **Which of these characteristics may reveal the coelacanth's adaptation to its deep ocean habitat? Tick as many as are applicable.**
   a. [   ] a fat-filled buoyancy organ
   b. [   ] a specially flexible jaw
   c. [   ] a possibly slow metabolism
   d. [   ] its large size
   e. [   ] its speed
   f. [   ] the possible ability to sense prey's electrical charges
   g. [   ] its colour

16. **What special characteristics did coelacanths and lung-fish have?**
   a. They had fins with skeletons and muscles.
   b. They were the first amphibians.
   c. They had slow metabolisms.
   d. They were adapted to the deep ocean.

✪ UNIT 4   The Hanging Gardens

Read the extract and answer the questions that follow.

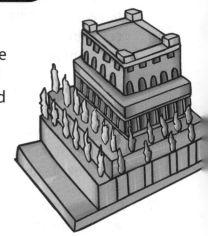

The Hanging Gardens of Babylon, located on the east bank of the Euphrates about 50 kilometres from the present city of Baghdad in Iraq, were an annex to the original royal palace, and comprised a series of terraces, supported by arcades. These had brick and bitumen walls seven metres thick, with passageways between them three metres wide and were as high as the city walls (30 metres or 100 metres, depending on which book is read). The terraces were constructed by placing an initial layer of reeds mixed with a large quantity of bitumen, then a double course of baked bricks bonded with cement and topped by sheets of lead. The waterproofing was essential; otherwise, the bricks would dissolve when the Gardens were irrigated. Soil was piled on top and various grasses and shrubs planted. The plants were kept constantly moist by means of hidden water-screws which pumped water up from the river, Euphrates.

The Gardens were built by King Nebuchadnezzar II, and the story goes that he did this to placate his Persian wife, Amyitis, who, when she looked out on the flat, dusty terrain of Mesopotamia, was homesick for the flowers and trees of her native land. Artificial gardens were not common in the ancient world.

The Hanging Gardens were extensively described by Strabo and Diodorus Siculus, prominent Greek historians of the day. However, Herodotus, who admires the impressive Walls of Babylon, another wonder of the time, makes no mention of the Gardens at all. Neither do the Babylonian records of the time contain any mention of them. Archaeologists believed that they had found the foundations of the Gardens, but later changed their minds when it became obvious that the area had only been storage facilities for the palace. It is possible that through the ages the location of the Gardens may have been confused with gardens that did actually exist at Ninevah, of which there is ample evidence in old books.

1. **The meaning of 'initial' –**
   a. solid
   b. supple
   c. long-lasting
   d. primary

2. **In their time the Gardens would have been –**
   a. like many other gardens
   b. inferior to the Ninevah Gardens
   c. a source of wonder
   d. something to be hidden

3. **The countryside around Babylon was likely to have been –**
   a. heavily populated
   b. mountainous with lush vegetation
   c. full of artificial gardens
   d. desert-like

4. **What can be inferred from the use of the word 'placate' in the second paragraph?**
   a. That Amyitis was a keen gardener.
   b. That Nebuchadnezzar wished to impress her Persian relatives.
   c. That Amyitis' unhappiness was causing problems.
   d. That Amyitis detested the Babylonians.

5. **The inclusion of lead in the construction was essential –**
   a. to strengthen the walls
   b. to secure the bricks
   c. to limit the size of the plants
   d. to waterproof the structure

6. **Which of these statements is true?**
   a. The Gardens were later converted into storage.
   b. The Gardens at Ninevah were larger.
   c. Strabo and Herodotus wrote about the Gardens.
   d. Mesopotamia is now named Iraq.

7. **Which statement is false?**
   a. The exact height of the Gardens is not known.
   b. Rain was infrequent in Mesopotamia.
   c. Many ancient cities had artificial gardens.
   d. The palace at Babylon has been excavated.

8. **Which of these statements can be inferred from the text?**
   a. The construction of the Gardens would have taken many years.
   b. There may not have actually been any gardens at Babylon.
   c. Herodotus did not think the Gardens were worth mentioning.
   d. Archaeologists will certainly solve the puzzle of the Gardens.

9. **Which of these words can replace 'terrain'?**
   a. desert
   b. woodlands
   c. landscape
   d. metropolis

10. **Which of these was not a historian?**
    a. Strabo
    b. Diodorus
    c. Amyitis
    d. Herodotus

11. **Which of these phrases could be substituted for 'ample evidence'?**
    a. scanty data
    b. abundant documentation
    c. mythical accounts
    d. scattered solitary facts

12. **Which evidence in the passage supports the description of the Walls of Babylon as 'impressive'?**
    a. their indestructibility
    b. their age
    c. their solid construction
    d. their height

13. **A 'double course' would be**
    a. Two servings of dinner.
    b. An extra thick layer.
    c. Special types of bricks.
    d. Two layers.

14. **Which of these words cannot be substituted for 'obvious'?**
    a. clear
    b. vague
    c. noticeable
    d. apparent

Read the extract and answer the questions that follow.

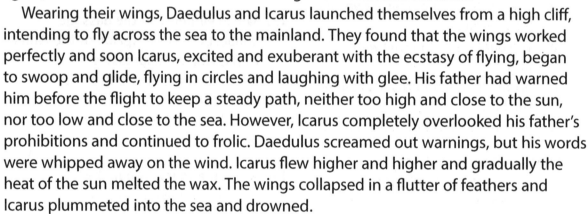

Once there was a clever craftsman in Athens named Daedulus. He worked skilfully with wood and was credited with creating many of the techniques of carpentry. However, he killed his nephew, Talos, who was also his apprentice because the young man had invented the saw. Daedulus and his son, Icarus, were obliged to flee Athens and to seek refuge on the island of Crete.

In Crete, Daedulus was initially very popular for his clever and well-made constructions. He designed and built a labyrinth to imprison the Minotaur, the half-bull, half-man monster son of the king, Minos. But, he fell from favour when he later assisted an enemy of the king to kill the Minotaur. Realising that he and his son needed to flee for their lives again, Daedulus fashioned two sets of wings from wax and feathers.

Wearing their wings, Daedulus and Icarus launched themselves from a high cliff, intending to fly across the sea to the mainland. They found that the wings worked perfectly and soon Icarus, excited and exuberant with the ecstasy of flying, began to swoop and glide, flying in circles and laughing with glee. His father had warned him before the flight to keep a steady path, neither too high and close to the sun, nor too low and close to the sea. However, Icarus completely overlooked his father's prohibitions and continued to frolic. Daedulus screamed out warnings, but his words were whipped away on the wind. Icarus flew higher and higher and gradually the heat of the sun melted the wax. The wings collapsed in a flutter of feathers and Icarus plummeted into the sea and drowned.

1. **Which of these phrases has a similar meaning to 'credited with creating'?**
   a. claimed to have discovered the methods
   b. instructed in the techniques
   c. acknowledged for the procedures
   d. received payment for the skills

2. **The first paragraph suggests that Daedulus was**
   a. original and steady
   b. ingenious, but jealous
   c. envious, but mild
   d. envious and flighty

3. **Which of these phrases tell the reader that this is not a factual recount?**
   a. his father's prohibitions
   b. two sets of wings
   c. half-bull, half-man
   d. the ecstasy of flying

4. **Daedulus lost the goodwill of the king**
   a. because he killed Talos, his nephew
   b. because he imprisoned the king's son, the Minotaur
   c. because he attempted to flee from Crete
   d. because he aided in the slaughter of the monster

5. An antonym for 'prohibition' is
   a. acquiescence
   b. embargo
   c. threat
   d. chastisement

6. 'Excited and exuberant with the ecstasy of flying' is an example of
   a. a metaphor
   b. informal language
   c. alliteration
   d. a pun

7. This legend is often seen as a warning not to be
   a. deceitful
   b. malicious
   c. hasty
   d. overambitious

8. How many examples of alliteration are there in the text?
   a. three
   b. four
   c. five
   d. six

9. Which of these statements is true?
   a. Talos and Icarus were cousins.
   b. The wings were made of waxed feathers.
   c. Daedulus built sections of the king's palace
   d. Daedulus intended to fly to another island

10. Which statement is false?
   a. Daedulus built a prison for the Minotaur.
   b. Daedulus hired someone to kill the Minotaur.
   c. The monster's death was caused by Minos' enemy.
   d. Minos was likely to execute Daedulus for his part in the Minotaur's death.

11. Which words reveal Icarus' delight in flying?
   a. the ecstasy of flying
   b. worked perfectly
   c. a steady path
   d. laughing with glee

12. Why did Icarus ignore the instructions Daedulus gave him before flying?
   a. He was a disobedient boy.
   b. The wind whipped the words away.
   c. He didn't trust his father.
   d. He became too absorbed in the experience.

13. A word which is most nearly opposite to 'prohibition' is
   a. go-ahead
   b. go over
   c. go off
   d. go into

14. 'Plummeted' means
   a. glided downwards
   b. drifted down gradually
   c. submerged
   d. fell like a stone

15. Which fact cannot be found in the text?
   a. Crete is an island.
   b. Athens was close to Crete.
   c. Talos had lived in Athens.
   d. Daedulus originally enjoyed respect in Crete.

16. The main purpose of the legend is to
   a. persuade
   b. entertain
   c. teach a lesson
   d. tell a story

⊗ UNIT 6   Going, Going, Gone

Read the extract and answer the questions that follow.

What do the Saiga Antelope of the Eurasian steppes, the Harpy Eagle of South America, the Pygmy Mouse Lemur of Madagascar and our own Tasmanian Devil have in common? Their populations are fast dwindling and they are all in imminent danger of becoming extinct.

Only twenty years ago, there were millions of Saiga Antelopes. Nowadays, there are only about 50 000 of these fleet-footed animals. This is partly due to loss of habitat, disease and drought. However, their greatest danger has come from poachers who have killed them for their horns which are believed in some cultures to have medicinal properties. Saiga Antelopes are characterised by their humped noses which filter out the dust of their arid homes in semi-desert steppes and grasslands.

Numbered among the world's largest birds of prey, Harpy Eagles can weigh up to 9 kilos and have wingspans measuring 2 metres. The Eagles' habitat is dense forest, where they seek tree-dwelling prey such as monkeys, birds, sloths, possums and small reptiles. Logging and invasion of the forest by farming has reduced the area of the Eagles' habitat and as a result, their numbers.

The Pygmy Mouse Lemur is the world's smallest primate and weighs only 30 grams. These shy little creatures live in female-dominated groups of up to fifteen animals. The habitat of these forest dwellers is also under threat because of human activities. As well, the lemurs are eagerly sought for the illegal trade in exotic pets.

The Tasmanian Devil is the world's largest carnivorous marsupial. It hunts fish, mice and small birds, scavenges carrion and will also ferret through household scraps in campgrounds or in domestic rubbish bins. It has a most alarmingly loud screech as well as having a mouth like a steel trap! It has the strongest bite for its size of any living mammal. The threat to the Devil Population is disease. For the last ten years, a rare and contagious cancer (Devil Facial Tumour Disease) has drastically reduced Devil numbers.

1. The Devil has 'a mouth like a steel trap'. This is an example of -
   a. a metaphor
   b. a simile
   c. technical language
   d. personification

2. 'A mouth like a steel trap' suggests
   a. it eats only fresh kill
   b. it is large for its size
   c. its eats quickly
   d. its bite is savage

3. **A synonym for 'arid' is**
   a. luxuriant
   b. parched
   c. flat
   d. withering

4. **Which are hunted commercially?**
   a. the eagle and the lemur
   b. the antelope and the Devil
   c. the lemur and the antelope
   d. the Devil and the eagle

5. **The Devil is at risk**
   a. from overpopulation
   b. from disease
   c. from poaching
   d. from loss of its habitat

6. **Read these statements about the Devil's diet.**
   (i) It will only eat live kill.
   (ii) It is carnivorous.
   (iii) It is omnivorous.
   (iv) It will eat whatever is available.
   Which two of these statements are true?
   a. (i) and (ii)
   b. (ii) and (iii)
   c. (ii) and (iv)
   d. (iii) and (iv)

7. **Which feature of one of the animals reveals adaptation to its environment?**
   a. The Devil's screech.
   b. The lemur's size.
   c. The eagle's wingspan.
   d. The antelope's nose

8. **Which statement is true?**
   a. Saiga Antelopes and Pygmy Mouse Lemurs live in groups.
   b. Tasmanian Devils and Pygmy Mouse Lemurs are nocturnal.
   c. Harpy Eagles and Saiga Antelopes are herbivorous.
   d. Tasmanian Devils and Harpy Eagles are carnivorous.

9. **'Fleet-footed' is an example of**
   a. onomatopoeia
   b. exaggeration
   c. slang
   d. alliteration

10. **The Harpy Eagle's greatest threat is**
    a. poaching
    b. humans
    c. disease
    d. drought

11. **'Their horns which are believed to have medicinal properties...' From this we can infer**
    a. this belief is unrealistic
    b. this belief is an excuse for poachers' greed
    c. this belief is completely false
    d. this belief could be tested by research

12. **Which animal or bird could possibly be found in a high-class shopping mall?**
    a. the Harpy Eagle
    b. the Tasmanian Devil
    c. the Pygmy Mouse Lemur
    d. The Saiga Antelope

13. **Which word could be substituted for 'steppes' in the last sentence of the second paragraph?**
    a. lowlands
    b. stairways
    c. deserts
    d. peaks

14. **Which of these words cannot be substituted for 'contagious'?**
    a. infectious
    b. pandemic
    c. transferable
    d. catching

Read the extract and answer the questions that follow.

The Afghan Hound is featured in rock carvings dating from 2200 BC. Prized by hunters in those days, the breed is now raised to be companions and pets. The Afghan Hound belongs to the greyhound family, and can reach a metre in height and more than 25kg in weight. The fine coat is usually cream, fawn or golden, but never red. The dog was introduced into England by Captain John Barff in the early 20th century.

Another dog whose line stretches back into antiquity is the Basenji, native to the inner Congo basin. Egyptian rock carvings of between 4000 and 5000 years ago depict the breed exactly as it is today. Last century, the Basenji was still being used for hunting antelope by the natives of the Congo area. Their method was to tie gourds filled with pebbles around the dogs' necks in order to make as much noise as possible and startle the prey so that they made a movement. Domesticated Basenjis have moved beyond Africa to all other parts of the world. It is prized as a pet for its quiet nature.

The Borzoi, a favourite dog of the Russian royal court, fell out of favour after the Russian Revolution removed the royal family in the early twentieth century. This elegant dog, of at least a metre tall, was bred for wolf-hunting. Two Borzois working together were capable of bringing down a full-grown wolf. Today, the dog is bred for beauty and friendship, not for hunting, and its silky white coat, often marked with fawn, orange or red markings, is much admired in Britain, Europe and America, where it is known as the Russian Wolfhound.

The Chiahuahua is sometimes called the Mexican Dwarf Dog or the Ornament Dog. This tiny 'lap-dog', the darling of many indulgent owners, may weigh from 1 to 3 kg. The breed is descended from the Aztec Sacred Dog.

1. **The meaning of 'antiquity' is -**
    a. pedigree
    b. the far distant past
    c. distantly related dogs
    d. a couple of centuries past

2. **Which dog was used for hunting bears?**
    a. the Borzoi
    b. the Basenji
    c. the Russian Wolfhound
    d. none of them

3. **Which dog still hunted last century?**
    a. the Afghan Hound
    b. the Chihuahua
    c. the Basenji
    d. none of them

4. **Why did the Basenjis carry gourds filled with pebbles?**
   a. The natives were frightened of the antelopes.
   b. The noise would scare predators away.
   c. The hunters liked making a noise.
   d. The noise would scare the antelopes out of their hiding places.

5. **The Russian imperial court was**
   a. a law court
   b. the government
   c. the royal court
   d. upper-class homes

6. **Which dog may be red?**
   a. the Basenji
   b. the Afghan Hound
   c. the Borzoi
   d. none of them

7. **Which of these statements is likely to be true?**
   a. The Russian Wolfhound is a member of the greyhound family.
   b. Two Basenjis working together could bring down a wolf.
   c. The Basenji is quite unlike its ancestors.
   d. The Aztec Sacred Dog was also tiny.

8. **Why might the Afghan, Basenji and Borzoi not used for hunting now?**
   a. They have forgotten their hunting skills.
   b. Hunting is not such a popular activity now.
   c. The dogs are too expensive.
   d. Wolves are extinct.

9. **'Fell out of favour' means -**
   a. Borzois forgot how to hunt.
   b. Borzois became endangered.
   c. Borzois became less popular.
   d. Borzois were exported.

10. **Which of these statements about Basenjis is true?**
    a. The Basenji is native to the African continent.
    b. The Basenji features in rock paintings dating from more than 4000 years ago.
    c. The Basenji is still being used for hunting antelopes.
    d. The Basenji is at least one metre tall.

11. **Which of these statements about Borzois is false?**
    a. It was a co-operative and aggressive hunter.
    b. The dog was initially bred for beauty and friendship.
    c. It may have a white coat with orange markings.
    d. This dog was prized by the Russian royal family.

12. **What do you think a 'lap-dog' is likely to be?**
    a. A dog that has lapsed in favour.
    b. A dog that can run laps.
    c. A dog that laps up water.
    d. A dog that can fit comfortably on someone's lap.

13. **Which dog is prized for its serene disposition?**
    a. the Afghan Hound
    b. the Borzoi
    c. the Basenji
    d. the Aztec Sacred Dog

14. **The likely audience for this text would be**
    a. children and teenagers
    b. general readership
    c. dog owners
    d. historians

Read the extract and answer the questions that follow.

The acorn, designed to grow into a mighty oak tree, frequently becomes home to a miniature ecosystem of herbivores, carnivores, parasites and predators, and as a consequence, dies and decays, never fulfilling its destiny.

The first attack on an acorn usually comes from the Acorn Weevil, a centimetre-long creature of immense determination. Utilising minute teeth at the end of an elongated snout, the weevil chisels its way for many days through the tough skin of the acorn, consuming the nutmeat and creating a tiny channel which will be the nursery for her egg. When the egg hatches, the larva eats a larger cavity in the acorn, taking several weeks in the process until the acorn falls from the tree. This signals the adult larva to begin eating its way out, after which its digs underground and remains dormant for from one to five years.

Another insect which feeds on acorns is the Filbert Worm. However, these worms are, in turn, at risk from specialised parasites such as the Braconid Wasp, which lays its eggs inside those of the Filbert Worm. As the egg hatches and the host caterpillar grows, so does the parasite larva inside, until it eventually bursts out!

The holes created by the Acorn Weevil and the Filbert Worms may allow other creatures, known as secondary colonists, to enter. One of these, the Short-snouted Weevil, has a capacity for play-acting. If alarmed by something, it 'plays dead'. Fierce predators, such as tiny centipedes, roam through acorns, searching for prey which may take the form of tiny slugs, snails, beetles, mites or ants.

1. **'Dormant' means -**
    a. concealed
    b. inactive
    c. animated
    d. famished

2. **A synonym for 'capacity' as it is used here is -**
    a. contents
    b. craving
    c. ability
    d. weakness

3. **What does 'a tiny creature of immense determination' mean?**
    a. The Acorn Weevil fights off all other insects.
    b. Its teeth break easily while tunnelling through the acorn.
    c. It takes some months to tunnel into the acorn.
    d. Its tiny teeth gnaw persistently through the acorn's tough skin.

4. **From hatching out of the egg to its emerging from the earth can take an Acorn Weevil**
   a. several weeks
   b. several days
   c. less than a year
   d. several years

5. **What might 'a specialised parasite' be?**
   a. There are only a few of the species remaining.
   b. It depends on one other particular species to survive.
   c. Firm conclusions about these parasites are still being researched.
   d. It needs assistance to live and reproduce.

6. **The centipede is an example of which of these?**
   a. an arachnid
   b. a specialised parasite
   c. a secondary colonist
   d. a herbivore

7. **Which of these are not found in an acorn?**
   a. ants
   b. spiders
   c. wasps
   d. centipedes

8. **Which of these statements is true?**
   a. The Braconid Wasp can feign death.
   b. The Acorn Weevil does not actually consume the acorn.
   c. The Filbert Worm preys on the Short-snouted Weevil.
   d. The Acorn Weevil has a lengthy nose.

9. **Which of these statements is false?**
   a. Few acorns actually germinate and grow into trees.
   b. The Acorn Weevil lays a single egg in an acorn.
   c. The Braconid Wasp lays eggs within the Filbert Worm caterpillar.
   d. Predators are always part of the food chain within an acorn.

10. **The purpose of this text is to**
    a. define
    b. enlighten
    c. convince
    d. divert

11. **'Never fulfilling its destiny' means**
    a. becoming a home to parasites
    b. dying and decaying
    c. failing to germinate and grow
    d. falling to the ground

12. **'Remains dormant for from one to five years' is an example of**
    a. a clause
    b. an unproven statement
    c. a phrase
    d. the author's viewpoint

13. **In which of these books might this text be found?**
    a. 'Tiny Carnivores.'
    b. 'Fascinating Ecosystems.'
    c. 'Insect Actors.'
    d. 'Weevils and Wasps.'

Read the extract and answer the questions that follow.

Men have been shaving off their beards for at least 30 000 years. In the Stone Age, they used the ancient equivalent of the modern disposable razor. A sharpened shell or piece of flint, or a shark's tooth all served the purpose. The Aztecs used pieces of volcanic glass known as obsidian, while archaeologists in Europe, India and Egypt have discovered blades of iron, bronze, gold and copper in ancient tombs.

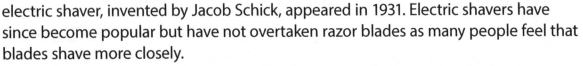

Razors became safer for their users in the 17th century with the invention of the first 'safety razor' by a Frenchman, Jean-Jacques Perret. He added a metal grip to the blade. This razor became dull with use and needed frequent sharpening with a strop.

The next advance for shavers was the disposable blade. King Gilette takes the credit for creating very thin steel blades, and became a rich man when his sales climbed into the millions. The first electric shaver, invented by Jacob Schick, appeared in 1931. Electric shavers have since become popular but have not overtaken razor blades as many people feel that blades shave more closely.

Besides razors, men and women utilised a variety of other ways of removing unwanted hair. Ancient Greek ladies singed the hair off their legs – a dangerous practice! Romans engaged the services of a hair-plucker who would pull out hairs, one by one. Hot wax or abrasion with pumice stones were two other slightly less painful methods used by Roman 'beauticians'.

In modern times, waxing is still a common method of hair-removal. Two other ways available in beauty salons are electrolysis, in which an electric current is sent through the hair follicle to destroy the root. The same effect is achieved by laser hair removal, but with pulses of light. Most of these methods involve some degree of discomfort.

1. The meaning of 'abrasion' is
   a. shaving
   b. heating
   c. scraping
   d. plucking

2. Why were Stone Age razors equally as disposable as modern ones?
   a. They were also thin slivers of metal.
   b. They were fragile
   c. There was no lack of them.
   d. They didn't shave well.

3. **On which continent were glass razors used?**
   a. Europe
   b. South America
   c. Asia
   d. Africa

4. **Which ancient people used wax to remove hair?**
   a. Greeks
   b. Aztecs
   c. French
   d. Romans

5. **Electric shavers –**
   a. have gone out of fashion
   b. are seen by many as inferior to blades
   c. are regarded by most people as equally useful
   d. will eventually overtake blades in sales

6. **The text suggests that Ancient Romans**
   a. enjoyed personal attention.
   b. did not usually bother to shave.
   c. were willing to endure pain to achieve the desired look.
   d. felt metal blades were too dangerous.

7. **Which statement is true?**
   a. A Frenchman invented the first 'safety razor'.
   b. Schick invented the first fully disposable razor.
   c. Rubbing with pumice caused no discomfort at all.
   d. The invention of the disposable razor did not make its inventor rich.

8. **Gilette's invention was–**
   a. untimely
   b. unrealistic
   c. electrolysis
   d. lucrative

9. **The language in this text is**
   a. colloquial
   b. entertaining
   c. informative
   d. persuasive

10. **A device for sharpening razors is called**
    a. a pumice stone
    b. obsidian glass
    c. a flint
    d. a strop

11. **Why is 'beauticians' placed in inverted commas?**
    a. They were like their modern counterparts.
    b. These professionals were always found in Rome.
    c. They were unlike modern beauty specialists.
    d. Beauty therapists did not enjoy respect.

12. **If women 'singed' hair from their legs**
    a. they scratched it
    b. they scorched it
    c. they scalded it
    d. they scotched it

13. **Which sentence below most nearly matches the last section of the text?**
    a. All of these methods were uncomfortable.
    b. Some of these methods were not painful.
    c. None of these methods were completely painless.
    d. All of these methods were free from discomfort.

14. **A word which could replace 'follicle' is**
    a. hue
    b. base
    c. shaft
    d. tip

Read the extract and answer the questions that follow.

The first European pearling businesses were established on the coast of Western Australia in the middle of the 19th century, and immediately employed many Aborigines who were already skilled 'free divers'. (A free diver is one who can dive to quite significant depths without any scuba equipment.) The Aborigines collected oyster shells for the Europeans who sold the mother-of-pearl. After a time, the industry expanded greatly and many native people were forced to work. This appalling practice was termed 'blackbirding' and was often characterised by non-existent wages and ill-treatment of many kinds.

In the 1880's laws were passed, outlawing blackbirding, and the vacuum created by their departure was filled by many immigrants from Asia and the Pacific Island. It was the Japanese settlers who had a huge impact on the industry. Attired in canvas suits, lead boots and copper helmets, they were the mainstay of the industry for the next 50 years. They also knew the secret of 'seeding' pearls, but at this stage there was no interest

After World War Two, the pearling industry took a new direction. Before this, pearls had been a sideline while mother-of-pearl was the main commodity. However, mother-of-pearl diminished in appeal with the growth of plastics. In 1956, the first cultured-pearl farm was established on the Kimberley coast. Here, oysters were seeded with tiny beads which stimulated them to produce nacre, the raw material of pearls.

Now, there are at least twenty pearling companies maintaining farms on the W.A. coast. Usually, the oyster shells are collected at sea and brought to the farm to be seeded. Then, they are kept on racks in underwater farms, where they are regularly cleaned and turned. This is essential as marine growth can carry parasites which can kill the oysters. Japan is the world's largest producer of cultured pearls, but Australia makes the largest and the best quality pearls.

1. **The meaning of 'mainstay' is**
   a. leaders
   b. chief support
   c. transformers
   d. unpaid

2. **'Blackbirding' could be described as**
   a. slave labour
   b. justifiable
   c. unprofitable
   d. necessary

3. **Pearls became more important than mother-of-pearl**
   a. in the 1880's
   b. in the 20th century
   c. in the 19th century
   d. in 1956

4. **What is the main reason the pearling bosses might have practised 'blackbirding'?**
   a. The Aborigines were good divers.
   b. It ensured good profits.
   c. No-one else wanted to dive.
   d. There was no work for Aborigines.

5. **What does the first sentence of the second paragraph mean?**
   a. New vacuum technology was invented.
   b. Pearls were vacuumed up and divers were no longer needed.
   c. The Aborigines walked off the job.
   d. New divers from other countries were employed.

6. **What does "diminished in appeal" mean?**
   a. became more in demand
   b. became scarcer
   c. became less attractive
   d. became less valuable.

7. **Until the end of World War II –**
   a. Pearls were only a small part of the industry.
   b. Mother-of-pearl was not considered valuable.
   c. Both pearls in great numbers and mother-of-pearl were harvested.
   d. Many natural pearls were still being discovered.

8. **Which statement is true?**
   a. The Aboriginal divers wore canvas suits.
   b. Unless regularly cleaned, the oysters will die.
   c. The outer shell of the oyster is called "nacre".
   d. Japan produces the largest cultured pearls.

9. **Which sentence best expresses the idea of 'a sideline'?**
   a. Something which is no longer produced.
   b. An item of secondary importance.
   c. Something which is increasing in importance.
   d. The main item out of several produced.

10. **A 'commodity' is**
    a. a concern
    b. a requirement
    c. the material
    d. a product

11. **Which of these facts cannot be found in the text?**
    a. Australia produces the finest cultured pearls.
    b. Top quality pearls are expensive.
    c. The Japanese created the method for making cultured pearls.
    d. The first cultured pearl farm was set up more than sixty years ago.

12. **Which of these words is most nearly opposite in meaning to 'stimulated'?**
    a. obliged
    b. allowed
    c. suppressed
    d. requested

13. **'The rights of the workers were secondary to the greed of the bosses.' To which paragraph could this sentence be added?**
    a. first
    b. second
    c. third
    d. fourth

Read the extract and answer the questions that follow.

Much data about the behaviour of hurricanes is obtained by flying planes through the storm, dropping temperature probes as they go. The planes used are propeller driven aircraft which were once employed as submarine hunters. They were equipped then with missiles and depth charges. Nowadays, they carry a crew of

nine, a dozen scientists and a full cargo of radar gear and scientific instruments. They can fly for nine hours without needing to refuel.

When flying through the hurricane, it is essential to keep the wings level and to fly at just the right speed. If they fly too slowly, the wings will lose lift and the plane will plunge downwards; if they fly too fast, the wind will begin to tear parts of the fuselage off. It is never a smooth ride. The plane dips, rolls, rocks, sways, lurches and shudders.

If the hurricane is moving over water, as the plane progresses through the storm, scientists will drop temperature probes called drop sondes. The probes are about a metre long and are attached to a parachute. These will descend to the surface of the ocean, submerge and measure temperature to a depth of 300 metres, transmitting this information back to the plane. It is planned to experiment with dropping these probes into the ocean ahead of the storm. Knowing the temperature of the water will help forecasters to predict how intense the storm may be.

When hurricanes pass over water they leave huge pools of cooler water behind them. These pools may remain for a month, and could possibly have profound effects on climate which we do not yet completely understand.

1. **What is the best meaning for 'ahead of the storm'?**
   a. in each individual storm
   b. in the predicted path of the storm
   c. in the area surrounding the storm
   d. to prevent the storm

2. **The force of a hurricane**
   a. cannot be measured
   b. does not vary
   c. can be predicted
   d. cannot be predicted

3. **When the planes were used in wartime**
   a. the passengers always had a smooth ride
   b. they found submarines and destroyed them
   c. they flew very unsteadily
   d. they were involved in hurricane research

4. **The 'worst case scenario' if a plane flies too slowly is that**
   a. the wings might fall off
   b. it might dive into the ocean
   c. it might lose the hurricane
   d. it might lose the temperature probes

5. **The 'worst case scenario' if a plane flies too fast is that**
   a. it will become impossible to control
   b. it might get ahead of the hurricane
   c. it might begin to disintegrate
   d. the scientists will not be able to conduct their experiments

6. **Temperature probes**
   a. are dropped over both land and water
   b. are entirely different to drop sondes
   c. fall 300 metres to the water
   d. are dropped solely over water

7. **The pools of cool water**
   a. last a few days
   b. are unrelated to hurricanes
   c. may affect climate
   d. occur seasonally

8. **It is likely that**
   a. these planes will not be used for much longer
   b. knowledge about hurricanes will increase
   c. hurricanes will decrease in intensity
   d. this research will discontinue due to lack of funds

9. **Which of these words is not a synonym for 'profound'?**
   a. intense
   b. extreme
   c. acute
   d. superficial

10. **Which of these statements is true?**
    a. Planes used in hurricane research are equipped with depth charges.
    b. Keeping the wings of these planes level ensures a steady ride.
    c. Maintaining the right speed is essential to the safety of the planes.
    d. These planes never fly directly through a storm.

11. **Which of these statements is false?**
    a. Only probes dropped over land require parachutes.
    b. Pools of cool water last for up to a month.
    c. Drop sondes are a metre long.
    d. Hurricane spotting planes can carry more than a dozen people.

12. **'Transmitting the information' is an example of**
    a. scientific jargon
    b. informal usage
    c. a clause
    d. technical language

13. **Knowing the temperature of the water before a hurricane strikes**
    a. will reveal where the pools of cool water will develop
    b. will help forecast the severity of the hurricane
    c. will show the path the hurricane will take
    d. will reveal the duration of the hurricane

14. **Which is true of the planes involved in hurricane research?**
    a. Their interiors are cramped.
    b. They have jet engines.
    c. They will soon be taken out of service.
    d. Their fuel consumption is economical.

Read the extract and answer the questions that follow.

The number of tigers in India is fast dwindling. A recent study by a conservation organisation has revealed that the tiger population of the four central states of Madhya Pradesh, Maharashta, Chattisgarh and Rajasthan has fallen from 1000 in 2002 to about 500 today. The causes are the erosion of their habitat, poaching and the encroachment of humans into their environment.

In the early 20th century, there were 40 000 tigers in India. A count in 2002 estimated that there were about 3700 throughout the country. However, conservation groups suggested that the figure could be closer to 1500 and might even be as low as a few hundred. They placed the major blame for this decline on widespread organised poaching.

Methods for determining tiger numbers have become more sophisticated since 2002. The study in 2002 counted only pug marks or tracks. Modern methods involve a greater number of people (88 000) and use actual sightings from camera traps, together with dung and pug mark examinations.

The recent study was welcomed by conservation groups because it revealed the seriousness of the present situation and might serve as a 'wake-up call' for both politicians and the general population. The news of the dwindling numbers will probably encourage opposition to China's proposal to lift the international ban on trade in tiger parts. Although trade in dead tigers is illegal, a single tiger can bring $25 000 on the black market. Tiger parts are highly in demand for traditional medicine. Even a claw can fetch about $15. If the ban is lifted, it will probably be a death knell for the Indian tigers.

1. **The best meaning for 'encroachment of humans' is**
   a. hunting of tigers for sport
   b. trapping of tigers near villages
   c. more humans sharing tiger habitats
   d. trade in tiger parts

2. **Which one of these words is an antonym for 'dwindling'?**
   a. mushrooming
   b. diminishing
   c. supposed
   d. static

3. **The most recent study of tiger numbers showed that**
   a. only 500 tigers remain throughout India
   b. only 1500 remain in the four central states
   c. at least 3700 remain throughout India
   d. only 500 remain in the four central states

4. **According to conservation groups, the main cause for the decline in tiger numbers is**
   a. erosion of the landscape by agriculture
   b. lack of good breeding programs in zoos
   c. systematic illegal hunting for profit
   d. humans sharing the tigers' environment

5. **The numbers counted in 2002 could be**
   a. unreliable because they relied on eye-witness accounts
   b. unreliable because of the simple methods of counting
   c. reliable because they used camera traps
   d. unreliable because they only counted in four states

6. **It can be inferred (worked out) from the text that**
   a. conservation groups become worried unnecessarily
   b. a combination of methods will ensure a more accurate result
   c. the ban on trade in tiger parts should be lifted
   d. more hunting goes on in the four central states

7. **The meaning of a 'wake-up call' is**
   a. a reminder to get up early
   b. a push to action
   c. a piece of good news
   d. something of no interest

8. **A 'pug mark' is**
   a. a paw print
   b. a dropping
   c. an injury
   d. a tally mark

9. **Trade in tiger parts continues because**
   a. soon there will be no tigers
   b. it is very profitable
   c. it will soon be legal
   d. it will be banned soon

10. **The ban is enforced**
    a. in India
    b. in China
    c. world-wide
    d. only since 2002

11. **What will foster opposition to lifting the ban?**
    a. the demands of traditional medicine
    b. the report of declining numbers
    c. the seriousness of the situation
    d. the profits made from illegal trade

12. **What is the meaning of a death knell?**
    a. A stimulus to try to save something.
    b. An indication that tigers have become extinct.
    c. A signal that something is coming to an end.
    d. An expression of sadness.

13. **The study 'was welcomed by conservation groups' because**
    a. it showed the situation was improving
    b. it showed earlier studies were false
    c. it was based on more exact data
    d. it showed how bad the situation has become

Read the extract and answer the questions that follow.

Alligators, bearded dragon lizards and gila monsters are all reptiles which eat only three or four times a year. Scientists have been conducting studies on the gila monster, a pink and black lizard about 0.6metres long which makes its home in Mexico. They are interested in how these reptiles can digest their food so slowly that they can go for months between meals. This ability is probably a result of evolutionary processes.

It was discovered that the gila was able to do this because of a chemical compound, called exendin-4, in its saliva. This chemical is efficient in slowing digestion. It was quickly realised that this discovery could have implications in the medical world, particularly in the treatment of type 2 diabetes. The idea was that if the absorption of carbohydrates could be slowed down in the same way the gila monster digests its prey, this would be beneficial. The diabetes patient might be able to control their sugar levels without putting on excess weight. Obesity is often a side effect of conventional treatments for diabetes and contributes to the problems of the patient.

Pharmaceutical companies began tests to see if an artificial form of the chemical could be developed. This was ultimately successful, and an artificial injectable drug was produced. It is effective in inducing the pancreas to produce more insulin in response to increased blood sugar. This reduces the need for the patient taking extra insulin. As well, it slows digestion and reduces the patient's appetite.

As well as helping diabetics, this project has benefited the gila monster, an endangered species. The pharmaceutical company which developed the drug has contributed to a foundation set up to preserve the reptile. A good outcome all round!

1. **The word 'implications' could be replaced by**
    a. causes
    b. costs
    c. significance
    d. success

2. **An antonym for 'inducing' is**
    a. creating
    b. stimulating
    c. aiding
    d. inhibiting

3. **The virtue of exendin-4 in the gila monster's saliva is that**
    a. it compresses the digestive process
    b. it helps the reptile eat a wide variety of foods
    c. it extends the digestive process
    d. it produces more sugar in the reptile's blood

4. **What is the best explanation of the last sentence of the first paragraph?**
    a. Over time the reptile will begin to eat more frequently.
    b. The reptile's digestion has adapted to living conditions.
    c. The reptile will eventually die out because of this.
    d. Other reptiles may eventually develop this same ability.

5. **What are 'conventional treatments'?**
    a. Ones proven to be ineffective.
    b. Ones not usually used.
    c. Ones which have side effects.
    d. Commonly used ones.

6. **What does the new drug do?**
    a. It increases blood sugar in response to carbohydrates.
    b. It increases insulin in response to raised blood sugar.
    c. It increases carbohydrates in response to raised blood sugar.
    d. It increases insulin in response to lowered blood sugar.

7. **What does the phrase 'ultimately successful' suggest?**
    a. The trials were all very successful.
    b. The trials were initially very successful.
    c. Success came after a time of experimentation.
    d. The trials are still continuing.

8. **What does the last sentence mean?**
    a. The discovery helped other people besides diabetes patients..
    b. The reptiles themselves did not benefit, but humans did.
    c. The pharmaceutical companies made a lot of money.
    d. It was advantageous for both humans and gila monsters.

9. **What is the meaning of a 'side-effect'?**
    a. obesity
    b. a condition caused by medication
    c. a benefit of conventional treatments
    d. a condition aggravated by treatment

10. **Which phrase has a similar meaning to 'a good outcome'?**
    a. a productive partnership
    b. a moderate development
    c. a significant cause
    d. a beneficial result

11. **Which statement is true?**
    a. The gila monster is six metres long.
    b. The lizard can control its sugar levels.
    c. The gila monster has extendin-4 in its saliva.
    d. Without intervention, this lizard might vanish.

12. **The text can be classified as**
    a. a journal
    b. an editorial
    c. a report
    d. a discussion

Read and complete the cloze passage with words from the that follow.

The rocket was used as a (1) _____ even before gun-powder was invented. There are pictures in old (2) _____ showing rockets being used by Arabs, Chinese and Indian armies. By the 16th century, however, rockets (3) _____ _____ to be used as guns had been well developed, and were much more (4) _____ _____.

But in the 18th century, rockets began to come into favour again. Hydar Ali, a prince in Mysore, India, used rockets very (5) _____ in battles with the English. An English soldier, Sir William Congreve, was impressed by this success and began to experiment with the rockets used in fireworks.

He (6) _____ them so much that he could (7) _____ his rockets 2 000 metres.

Congreve's rockets were first tried out by the British Navy in 1805. After this, the British Army formed a rocket division, (8) _____ with one hundred rockets. Armies in other countries followed their lead. The Rocket Age had begun.

1. **a.** tool
   b. weapon
   c. help
   d. gun

2. **a.** films
   b. colours
   c. countries
   d. books

3. **a.** began
   b. ceased
   c. forbade
   d. continued

4. **a.** unreliable
   b. fun
   c. reliable
   d. expensive

5. **a.** uselessly
   b. slowly
   c. effectively
   d. happily

6. **a.** liked
   b. improved
   c. reduced
   d. trimmed

7. **a.** explode
   b. take
   c. project
   d. see

8. **a.** burdened
   b. heavy
   c. armed
   d. attached

9. **Tick only the statements which contain information from this text.**
   - a. [ ] Guns were a large part of an army's store of weapons by the 16th century.
   - b. [ ] Many large cannons were in use in the 16th century.
   - c. [ ] The rocket is an ancient invention.
   - d. [ ] Hyadir Ali had a large army in Mysore, India.
   - e. [ ] Sir William Congreve was an admiral in the British Navy.
   - f. [ ] Congreve's rockets were very effective.
   - g. [ ] The British Navy formed a rocket division in the early 19th century.
   - h. [ ] The rocket division was armed with a hundred rockets.
   - i. [ ] Rockets have been steadily improved since the 19th century.
   - j. [ ] Rockets form the basis of the space exploration program.

10. **A synonym for 'invented' is**
    - a. defined
    - b. derived
    - c. devout
    - d. devised

11. **A phrase with nearly the same meaning as 'impressed by this success' is**
    - a. carefree about this occurrence
    - b. admiring of this tactic
    - c. bewildered by this practice
    - d. dubious about this achievement

12. **Which of these phrases could be substituted for 'their lead'?**
    - a. their generals
    - b. their experiments
    - c. their daydreams
    - d. their example

13. **Which phrase has a similar meaning to 'tried out'?**
    - a. took a punt
    - b. cut to the chase
    - c. put to the test
    - d. showed the way

14. **A phrase opposite in meaning to 'come into favour' is**
    - a. become obsolete
    - b. become vital
    - c. become random
    - d. become significant

15. **In which of these books might you find this text?**
    - a. 'The History of the British Navy.'
    - b. 'The Story of Fireworks.'
    - c. 'Warfare Through the Ages.'
    - d. 'Good Ideas That Failed.'

16. **The aim of the text is to**
    - a. convince
    - b. enlighten
    - c. enthral
    - d. guide

17. **Pictures in old books are**
    - a. totally reliable evidence
    - b. evidence of good imagination
    - c. fairly reliable evidence
    - d. totally unreliable evidence

18. **Who was responsible for rockets coming into favour again?**
    - a. Hydar Ali
    - b. Sir William Congreve
    - c. Congreve and Ali
    - d. The Chinese, Arab and Indian armies

19. **When did the Rocket Age begin?**
    - a. 16th century
    - b. 17th century
    - c. 18th century
    - d. 19th century

Read and complete the cloze passage with words from the that follow.

One of our primitive ancestors' first hunting weapons was a sling, used for pitching (1) _____ at prey. As time went on, slings became bigger and better and came to be used in (2) _____. By the Middle Ages huge contraptions were being constructed which took weeks to move into position and hours to prepare to fire at some (3) _____ castle. Some of these machines could fire a (4) _____ weighing up to 100 kilograms a distance of more than 500 metres. This created sufficient force to breach the walls of the castle.

As well as stones, burning barrels of incendiary (5)_____ were sometimes hurled over the castle walls. Another trick used was to sling dead and rotting animals (6) _____ the enemy with the hope of causing (7) _____.

During the First World War, a British officer devised a spring-operated sling which would (8) _____ hand grenades over the trenches, a distance of about 100 metres. It needed four men to manage it and it worked very efficiently.

1.	a. mud	5.	a. fire
	b. fire		b. soldiers
	c. stones		c. material
	d. wildly		d. sparks
2.	a. hunting	6.	a. in
	b. warfare		b. between
	c. weapons		c. with
	d. towns		d. among
3.	a. unimportant	7.	a. noise
	b. old		b. disease
	c. small		c. odours
	d. besieged		d. injuries
4.	a. missile	8.	a. propel
	b. shot		b. load
	c. bullet		c. bring
	d. sling		d. have

9. **Tick only the statements which contain information from this text.**
   a. [ ] Slings are an ancient invention.
   b. [ ] A sling is mentioned in the Bible.
   c. [ ] Using a sling in warfare was time-consuming.
   d. [ ] Much of World War I was fought in the trenches.
   e. [ ] Early sling machines were built of wood.
   f. [ ] Poisoned food was sometimes flung over castle walls.
   g. [ ] Slings are no longer used in warfare.
   h. [ ] Dead animals were flung over castle walls.
   i. [ ] Slings were used to project burning objects over walls.
   j. [ ] Sieges of castles could last for years.

10. **A synonym for 'primitive' is**
    a. contemporary
    b. prevailing
    c. inexpert
    d. primordial

11. **A phrase with nearly the same meaning as 'to breach the walls'**
    a. to undermine the walls
    b. to fracture the walls
    c. to project over the walls
    d. to advance to the walls

12. **Which word has a similar meaning to 'contraptions'?**
    a. models
    b. weapons
    c. slings
    d. mechanisms

13. **Which word is opposite in meaning to 'ancestors' ?**
    a. forerunners
    b. successors
    c. mentors
    d. predecessors

14. **Which word is an antonym for 'efficiently'?**
    a. capably
    b. laboriously
    c. rapidly
    d. agreeably

15. **'Slings were the forerunners of cannons which could reduce castle walls to rubble.' To which paragraph could this sentence be added?**
    a. first
    b. second
    c. third
    d. none

16. **Which of these statements is false?**
    a. Slings took weeks to move into a position where they could be fired.
    b. Some medieval slings were massive.
    c. Slings were used in World War II.
    d. Some slings could fire a rock weighing 100 kilos a distance of 500 metres.

17. **In which of these books might this information be found?**
    a. 'Medieval Warfare.'
    b. 'A History of Weapons.'
    c. 'Ancient Hunters.'
    d. 'Military Strategies.'

18. **Which of these factors probably contributed to the end of huge Medieval slings?**
    a. the materials used
    b. the time-consuming operation
    c. their inaccuracy
    d. their unpredictable results

19. **'Incendiary material'**
    a. smells very bad
    b. is full of germs
    c. is disposable
    d. burns fiercely

Read the extract and answer the questions that follow.

Lichens look like plants but they are not plants. Scientists describe them as miniature ecosystems, as they are composed of two or three different partners. The most significant member of the partnership is a fungus. The other partners may be a colony of algae or of bacteria.

Lichens obtain their food by photosynthesis: using sunlight to build up carbohydrate reserves. Lichens can survive in the most inhospitable of environments. They are found growing on tombstones, on roofs and even on windows that are not habitually cleaned. They have the ability to do this because they contain nearly 600 chemicals, unique to lichens, which make them invulnerable to attacks by bacteria and discourage herbivores grazing on them.

Dyes made from lichens have been used all through history. Grey lichens scraped off Mediterranean coastal rocks were used to manufacture purple dyes for royal robes. Harris Tweed, made in Scotland, used lichen based dyes which made the material moth-proof. Native American Indians prized the bright yellow wolf lichen (Letharia vulpina) and traded fish oil for it. The dye is still used by Alaskan First Nation members to colour their dancing blankets. Wolf lichen was also used to make a medicinal tea, as well as lotions to treat skin irritations.

Reindeer lichen (Cladina stellaris) is an essential food for North American caribou and Eurasian reindeer. When snow covers the lichens, the animals will dig down as deep as a metre to reach them. People in the Arctic once ate reindeer lichens when food was scarce. However, they considered them a particular treat when reclaimed, in a fermented state, from the stomachs of caribou!

1. **A synonym for 'invulnerable' is**
   a. helpful
   b. impenetrable
   c. insecure
   d. prone

2. **'Fermented' means**
   a. rotting
   b. converted to alcohol
   c. harmful
   d. medicinal

3. **Lichens may best be described as**
   a. Special types of plants which have bacteria as part of them.
   b. Fungi which consume insects.
   c. A combination of different things.
   d. Algae growing on plants.

4. **The most important partner in a lichen is**
   a. sometimes a fungus.
   b. never a fungus.
   c. as often a colony of algae as a fungus.
   d. always a fungus.

5. **Lichens are able to survive in which kind of conditions?**
   a. Only in hospitable conditions.
   b. In conditions in which other plants would die.
   c. Where there are no herbivores to feed on them.
   d. Where they are not at risk of attacks by bacteria.

6. **The chemicals which make lichens very hardy**
   a. are found in a wide range of plants
   b. are sometimes found in algae
   c. are not found in other organisms besides lichens
   d. encourage herbivores to feed on them

7. **Which lichen was used in making medicines?**
   a. Cladina stellaris
   b. grey Mediterranean lichens
   c. lichens from Eurasia
   d. wolf lichen

8. **Which statement is true?**
   a. Royal purple dye was made from Letharia vulpina.
   b. Robes of royal purple were moth-proof.
   c. Fermented reindeer lichen is used on skin diseases.
   d. Dyes are still being manufactured from lichens.

9. **Rheindeer are found in**
   a. North America
   b. Europe and Asia
   c. Alaska
   d. only Europe

10. **'A particular treat' is**
    a. a remedy
    b. a reward
    c. an essential
    d. a delicacy

11. **'Windows that are not habitually cleaned' would be**
    a. not cleaned thoroughly
    b. not in need of cleaning
    c. not cleaned of lichen
    d. not cleaned routinely

12. **Which one of these statements is false?**
    a. Some lichen-based dyes protect cloth from moths.
    b. Caribou dig down more than a metre to reach lichen.
    c. Fish oil was traded for wolf lichen.
    d. Grey lichen grows near the Mediterranean Sea.

13. **An antonym for 'scarce' is**
    a. copious
    b. limited
    c. valuable
    d. non-existent

14. **A word with the same meaning as 'reclaimed' is**
    a. revisited
    b. redone
    c. realised
    d. recovered

15. **'An essential food' would be**
    a. particularly attractive to them
    b. scarce in winter
    c. their main source of sustenance
    d. rich in vitamins

16. **The language used in this text is**
    a. informal
    b. formal
    c. scientific
    d. jargon

Read the extract and answer the questions that follow.

Mice make good pets if you do not have much space to house a pet nor time to exercise an animal such as a dog or ferret. Setting up a home for mice is easy and relatively cheap, the animals themselves are inexpensive and their care takes little time.

Mice can be black, blue, chocolate, fawn, cream, silver or a mixture of these hues. (Lighter coloured mice tend to be less smelly.) Their fur can long or short.

Pet mice can live happily in a cage or a plastic or glass tank. It is important to keep mice warm, so provide wood shavings, or cotton wool so that they can make nests for themselves. This bedding will need to be changed three times a week. Mice like to be active, especially at night, so put some toys such as ladders, tubes or wheels in the mouse house. Electronic equipment such as TV remotes can cause distress to mice, so situate your mice some distance away from it.

The best food for your mice is commercial mouse mix from the pet shop. This should constitute 90% of their diet, and can be supplemented by oats, whole-meal toast, hard-boiled egg, meat scraps, green vegetables and cheese.

Mice are members of the rodent family, animals which are characterised by the possession of four sharp, continuously growing incisors. They must gnaw objects to keep the teeth from growing too long, so you need to provide such things as carrots or apples to meet this need. Mice, which have been bred as domestic pets for many years, have a short life span of two or three years, so be prepared for this fact.

When choosing your mice, remember that mice breed rapidly, so unless you are wishing to provide a good supply of baby mice for your local pet shop, then opt for two females. They will be gentle and will become quite tame if you handle them regularly.

1. 'Relatively cheap' means
   a. not cheap
   b. exceptionally cheap
   c. moderately cheap
   d. somewhat expensive

2. What is the purpose of the information in brackets in the second paragraph?
   a. To show that males and females are different.
   b. To simply add more information.
   c. To show what most people think about this.
   d. To keep in mind when choosing a mouse.

3. **The text ranks these elements in which order of importance?**
   a. Cleanliness, warmth and toys.
   b. Toys, food and warmth.
   c. Warmth, cleanliness and toys.
   d. Privacy, warmth and cleanliness.

4. **The meaning of 'characterised by' is**
   a. hampered by
   b. distinguished by
   c. aided by
   d. illustrated by

5. **What is the purpose of the last sentence in the fifth paragraph?**
   a. To encourage you to reconsider keeping mice.
   b. To tell you to be careful to buy healthy mice.
   c. To prepare you for a short relationship with your pet.
   d. To advise you to look after your mice very carefully.

6. **Which of these statements is true?**
   a. Two male mice will be a good choice.
   b. Mice should never be given cheese.
   c. Wood shavings will help to keep the mice warm.
   d. Mice have only been bred domestically in recent years.

7. **Which of these should make up the bulk of the mouse's food?**
   a. fruit and vegetables
   b. eggs and cheese
   c. whole-meal food
   d. commercial food

8. **Which of these is an antonym for 'distress'?**
   a. anguish
   b. contentment
   c. harm
   d. reverberation

9. **What is 'this need' in the fourth paragraph?**
   a. The necessity of gnawing on something to prevent excessive growth of teeth.
   b. Allowing their teeth to grow which needs careful attention.
   c. The essential inclusion of apples and carrots in their diet.
   d. The need to be prepared for mice having a short life span.

10. **'Opt for' in the last paragraph can be replaced by**
    a. go over
    b. go into
    c. go by
    d. go for

11. **Which of these facts cannot be found in the text?**
    a. Dark brown mice would be smellier than white mice.
    b. Too much cheese will give mice a stomach-ache.
    c. Mice can live well in a fish tank.
    d. Mice can eat toast.

12. **Which statement could be made about mice as pets?**
    a. Mice are inexpensive, but high maintenance.
    b. Mice are low maintenance pets, but setting up can be quite expensive.
    c. Mice are inexpensive and low maintenance.
    d. Mice are only suitable pets if you don't have much space.

13. **'Pet mice can live happily ...' 'Happily' can be replaced by**
    a. safely
    b. joyfully
    c. blissfully
    d. comfortably

Read the extract and answer the questions that follow.

In old books, there are frightening pictures of giant octopuses wrapping their tentacles around ships and dragging them down to the watery depths. It is probably this myth which gave rise to one of the names of the giant octopus which is 'devilfish'. In fact, octopuses are intelligent and shy creatures which make excellent parents.

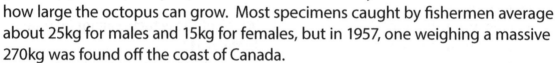

The octopus is a carnivorous marine mollusc belonging to the group known as cephalopods, and has a soft, rounded body with eight tentacles each bearing two rows of suckers. Its head has a beaklike mouth and on occasion, when provoked, octopuses (or octopi) have bitten people. It is not known exactly how large the octopus can grow. Most specimens caught by fishermen average about 25kg for males and 15kg for females, but in 1957, one weighing a massive 270kg was found off the coast of Canada.

The octopus moves by sucking water into its mantle, the baglike container for its internal organs and projecting it out through a syphon. In this way, it glides across the sea floor. When it spies likely prey such as a crab, it drops down on it, enveloping it and releasing poison into the water which immobilises the crab. Then, it uses its beak to crack the shell and reach the meat. An octopus can scoop up a number of stunned crabs in its web, the skin between its tentacles, and transport them back to its den.

Octopuses will eat near relatives such as abalone and have been known to eat other octopuses. When they are stressed – for example, in captivity – they will gnaw off their own arms which do grow back after a time! The tentacles can also break off as the octopus flees from predators such as whales, dolphins, seals, sea lions and various types of fish. A protective strategy used by octopuses is to squirt out a blackish ink which swirls around in the water, confusing the enemy while the octopus escapes.

1. **The octopus may be known as the 'devilfish'.**
   a. because it is very intelligent
   b. because it lurks in caves
   c. because of old stories which tell of it attacking ships
   d. because it is proven to have attacked ships.

2. **Giant octopuses usually grow**
   a. to more than 250kg
   b. to about 25kg for males and more for females
   c. to about 15kg for females but there is no upper limit for males
   d. from 15kg (females) to 25kg (males)

3. **The body of the octopus is called**
   a. the web
   b. the siphon
   c. the mantle
   d. the abdomen

4. **The octopus catches its prey**
   a. by attacking with its beak
   b. by paralysing them
   c. by choking them
   d. by taking them to its cave

5. **Octopuses may chew off their own tentacles**
   a. when they feel threatened by a predator
   b. when there are no other food sources
   c. when they are very upset
   d. so that new arms may grow in their place

6. **Which is the best meaning for the expression 'gave rise to'?**
   a. resulted in
   b. proved
   c. showed to be untrue
   d. gave a false impression

7. **The octopus is often able to escape from predators by**
   a. hiding in its cave most of the time
   b. darkening the water so it is unclear where the octopus is
   c. crushing them by wrapping its tentacles around them
   d. paralysing them with poison

8. **Which of these statements is true?**
   a. Octopuses like to eat abalone, crab and small seals.
   b. The plural of octopus can also be 'octopi'.
   c. No octopuses larger than 250kg have been found.
   d. Octopuses never eat their own kind.

9. **Which of these statements is false?**
   a. Sea lions prey on octopuses.
   b. Only in myths do octopuses attack ships.
   c. Octopuses never attack people.
   d. The octopus is a good parent.

10. **The octopus would move**
   a. clumsily
   b. effortlessly
   c. infrequently
   d. laboriously

11. **The best explanation of 'a protective strategy' is**
   a. a plan to safeguard itself
   b. a trick to fool prey
   c. an indication of its shy nature
   d. a sign of the octopus's intelligence

12. **The tentacles of the octopus _____ if lost.**
   a. reproduce
   b. repel
   c. relocate
   d. redevelop

13. **In which book might you find this text?**
   a. 'Myths of the Deep.'
   b. 'Protective Behaviour of Sea Creatures.'
   c. 'Colossal Cephalopods.'
   d. 'Captivating Critters.'

14. **'The baglike container for its internal organs' is an example of**
   a. informal expression
   b. figurative language
   c. inexact expression
   d. technical language

Read the extract and answer the questions that follow.

Jim Robbins was a twelve-year-old cabin boy on the Royal Navy ship, *Victory* in the early 19th century. His life, which was very different from yours, was full of hard work, difficult conditions and danger. He slept in a hammock strung from the ceiling beams, and almost touching the hammock next to him. His total personal space was about 40cm in total.

Rolling out of his hammock when it was time for his watch was very difficult at times and Jim had once been tempted to stay there just a few moments more. The punishment he received, of six cuts with a rattan cane, had convinced him of the need to leap out of bed as soon as the whistle blew. Although the pain of the cane had been fierce, the punishment

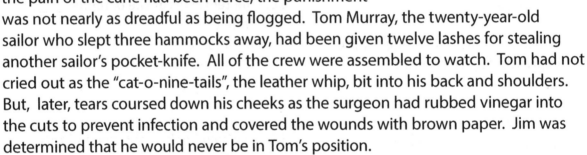

was not nearly as dreadful as being flogged. Tom Murray, the twenty-year-old sailor who slept three hammocks away, had been given twelve lashes for stealing another sailor's pocket-knife. All of the crew were assembled to watch. Tom had not cried out as the "cat-o-nine-tails", the leather whip, bit into his back and shoulders. But, later, tears coursed down his cheeks as the surgeon had rubbed vinegar into the cuts to prevent infection and covered the wounds with brown paper. Jim was determined that he would never be in Tom's position.

You would not have enjoyed the food Jim had to eat. For breakfast, he had cold porridge and "Scotch coffee" which was a mixture of crumbled ship's biscuits, hot water and molasses. For lunch, he had a stew made from salted pork or salted fish, and dried vegetables. (There were no refrigerators on board.) Dinner was hard biscuits, butter and cheese. However, the biscuits would have been full of weevils, the butter rancid and the cheese green with mould. Jim had quickly learned to bang his biscuits on the table to try to dislodge the weevils. Jim was also given lime juice to prevent scurvy from lack of vitamin C.

1. **Conditions on the 'Victory' were**
   a. cozy
   b. comfortable
   c. cramped
   d. cool

2. **'Flogged' means**
   a. cautioned
   b. shamed
   c. punished
   d. whipped

      ©Therese Burgess Five Senses Education Pty Ltd

3. **What conclusion can be drawn from the text?**
   a. Boys were given more food than the men were.
   b. Boys were not punished as severely as the men were.
   c. The crew enjoyed watching the floggings.
   d. Caning was a much worse punishment than was flogging.

4. **Why might the meat be salted and the vegetables dried?**
   a. It says the crew preferred them that way.
   b. There was no way of keeping food fresh in those days.
   c. It was difficult for the cook to prepare meals for so many.
   d. The salt would prevent scurvy.

5. **What sentence can be added to paragraph three?**
   a. As a hardworking and growing boy, Jim was often hungry.
   b. Jim made sure he got up as soon as the whistle blew.
   c. "Scotch coffee" was a nourishing and warming drink.
   d. Jim quickly learned to eat the weevils and not complain.

6. **Which fact cannot be found in the text?**
   a. The 'Victory' was involved in many battles.
   b. Cheese grew mould because it was not refrigerated.
   c. Jim was sometimes in dangerous situations.
   d. Vinegar was used to disinfect wounds.

7. **What was Jim's resolution?**
   a. To eat all of his food.
   b. To refrain from stealing.
   c. To get up quickly in the morning.
   d. To stay on the ship.

8. **What is the meaning of 'tears coursed down his cheeks'?**
   a. tears filled his eyes
   b. tears edged down his cheeks
   c. tears flowed like a river
   d. tears oozed down his cheeks

9. **What did Jim quickly learn to do?**
   a. take punishment without crying
   b. bang his biscuits to get rid of the weevils
   c. drink 'Scotch coffee'
   d. put vinegar on cuts to disinfect them

10. **'The cat-o-nine-tails…bit' is an example of**
    a. a metaphor
    b. exaggeration
    c. personification
    d. informal language

11. **'His total personal space' was**
    a. his space on the deck
    b. the cupboard in which he kept his possessions
    c. a place where he could be on his own
    d. slightly more than the width of his hammock

12. **If butter was 'rancid', it would**
    a. be rationed
    b. be full of weevils
    c. smell and taste awful
    d. be melting

13. **A word which could replace 'dislodge' is**
    a. disinfect
    b. slay
    c. displace
    d. crush

14. **'Lack of' means**
    a. a surplus
    b. insufficient
    c. the effects of
    d. the condition of

Read the extract and answer the questions that follow.

The Snowy River Scheme is a large hydro-electricity and irrigation complex in south eastern Australia. It covers more than 5000 square kilometers and is situated almost entirely within the Kosciuszko National Park. The Scheme comprises sixteen dams, a pumping station, seven power stations and two hundred and twenty kilometres of pipelines, aqueducts and tunnels. It was commenced in 1949 and finished in 1964, at a cost of $820 million. (At today's rates that would be $6 billion!) The chief engineer of this, the most massive engineering project ever attempted in Australia, was Sir William Hudson.

The principal underlying the Scheme was the capture of water in the high country of the Snowy Mountains and its diversion inland to the Murray and Murrumbidgee Rivers through two major tunnel systems drilled through the solid granite rock of the mountains. On its journey, the water falls 800 metres and travels through the various hydro-electric power stations which generate power for the ACT, New South Wales and Victoria. Providing 10% of all energy needs for New South Wales, the Scheme is the largest renewable energy producer on the mainland of Australia as well as one of the largest and most complex in the world. It also boosts the water flow in the Murray-Darling basin, allowing irrigation of crops.

One hundred thousand workers were employed from over thirty (mainly European) countries. Not only did the scheme provide well-paid work for migrants fleeing their war-torn homes in Europe, but they had a significant impact subsequently on the cultural mix of the population. Temporary towns were built to house workers and their families, and dismantled when that stage of construction was completed. Two of these, Cabramurra and Khancoban, have remained. Three towns, Adaminaby, Talbingo and Jindabyne, were inundated when new lakes (Eucumbene, Talbingo and Jindabyne) were created.

1. **A 'diversion' in the second paragraph is**
   a. transport
   b. amusement
   c. a detour
   d. utilisation

2. **The Snowy Scheme comprises**
   a. six dams, a pumping station and seven power stations
   b. seven pumping stations, sixteen dams and a power station
   c. a pumping station, seven power stations and sixteen dams
   d. seventeen dams, a pumping station and six power stations

3. **The Scheme improves water flow for**
   a. the Murrumbidgee River
   b. all of south eastern Australia
   c. the Snowy Mountains
   d. the Murray-Darling Basin

4. **The Scheme provides water for power in**
   a. New South Wales, the ACT and South Australia
   b. New South Wales, South Australia and Victoria
   c. the ACT, Victoria and New South Wales
   d. South Australia, the ACT and Victoria

5. **Which of these statements is true?**
   a. The Scheme would cost $820 million to build today.
   b. The Scheme supplies one tenth of NSW's energy needs.
   c. The water travels 80 kilometres through the mountains.
   d. The Scheme covers two hundred and twenty square kilometres.

6. **Which of these temporary towns exists today?**
   a. Adaminaby
   b. Eucumbene
   c. Cabramurra
   d. Jindabyne

7. **What is the significance of the Snowy Scheme? Tick as many of these boxes as are relevant.**
   a. [   ] Its massive size.
   b. [   ] How long it took to build.
   c. [   ] Its contribution to multiculturalism.
   d. [   ] It provides all of Victoria's energy needs.
   e. [   ] The tunneling was through granite.
   f. [   ] It is the largest renewable energy provider in Australia.

8. **Another word for 'inundated' is**
   a. dismantled
   b. swamped
   c. created
   d. designed

9. **Which of these can be substituted for 'boosts'?**
   a. regulates
   b. pays for
   c. heightens
   d. repairs

10. **This text could form part of**
    a. a newspaper article
    b. a textbook
    c. an encyclopaedia
    d. all of the above

11. **Which of these facts cannot be found in the text?**
    a. Cabramurra was originally a temporary town.
    b. New towns of Adaminaby, Talbingo and Jindabyne were created.
    c. Lake Eucumbene is a new lake created by the Scheme.
    d. Temporary towns housed workers and their families.

12. **'Allowing irrigation of crops' is an example of**
    a. a phrase
    b. a clause
    c. a verb group
    d. a compound sentence

13. **A word which is not a synonym for 'boosts' is**
    a. increases
    b. drains
    c. advances
    d. enhances

✪ UNIT 21 King Arthur – a Real Person?

Read the extract and answer the questions that follow.

The legend of King Arthur has come to us in countless retellings, all attesting to a gallant and courageous man, the very model of what a king should be like. The most famous and enduring version of the King Arthur story is "Morte d'Arthur", written by Thomas Mallory in the 15th century. However, over 13 000 other books and articles have been written about this charismatic character.

Arthur created a Round Table for his knights so that when they had a meeting, none enjoyed greater status than another. This was a democratic way of acting and because of this we regard Arthur as particularly enlightened for his times. Arthur's knights of the Round Table were expected to be men of upright character, who did good deeds and saved fair damsels (ladies) in distress. All had to strive to be kind and brave.

Arthur's castle was called "Camelot" and this name has come to mean an ideal place or even a wonderful period of time. In modern times, it was applied to the times of the US president, John Kennedy. In the Arthurian legends, the king was aided in all his endeavours by a mighty wizard, Merlin, who could change his shape at will into a bird, a deer or even a rabbit.

Was there really a King Arthur or not? There is some historic evidence that a charismatic king lived in England in the 5th or 6th century and was active against the Saxons. Whatever the truth of the matter, the story of Arthur continues to appeal to new generations. The universal theme of good winning over evil is part of this, as is the character of Arthur – good, brave and just.

1. **Which of these words could replace 'attesting to' in the first sentence?**
   a. disproving
   b. examining
   c. written by
   d. demonstrating

2. **An 'enduring version' is**
   a. a very long one
   b. one which is still appealing
   c. one with a message
   d. a true one

3. **The text suggests that Arthur**
   a. was something of a tyrant
   b. was an excellent soldier
   c. was advanced in his thinking
   d. was related to Merlin

4. **The use of 'Camelot' to refer to Kennedy's presidency is**
   a. derogatory
   b. complimentary
   c. descriptive
   d. feasible

5. Arthur is described twice as 'charismatic'. Which of the words below is the best synonym for this word?
   a. legendary
   b. captivating
   c. valiant
   d. good

6. Which of these statements is true?
   a. Merlin and Arthur ruled the country jointly.
   b. 'Morte d'Arthur' was written in the 13th century.
   c. Knights were expected to be protective of women.
   d. Camelot was built in the 5th century.

7. Which of these conclusions does the text not support?
   a. Arthur was supported by his knights.
   b. Arthur had high standards for his knights.
   c. People will continue to be fascinated by the Arthur legend.
   d. Merlin had a great deal of influence over Arthur.

8. 'Was there really a King Arthur or not?' This is an example of
   a. the author's viewpoint
   b. a request for information
   c. an expression of doubt
   d. a rhetorical question

9. The writer's point of view on Arthur is
   a. It will never be possible to prove if there was an Arthur or not.
   b. There is no evidence that Arthur was a historical figure.
   c. It is quite possible that Arthur really existed.
   d. It is extremely likely that Arthur was a real person.

10. In the last sentence,' this' refers to
    a. the universal theme
    b. the Arthurian legend
    c. Arthur's character
    d. Arthur's appeal

11. Which is the correct meaning for 'at will'?
    a. by exerting his will
    b. as he wished
    c. very willingly
    d. in a flash

12. Why is Arthur regarded as 'enlightened'?
    a. His expectations for his knights were high.
    b. He imposed a code of conduct on his knights.
    c. He created a democratic 'Round Table'.
    d. He was a charismatic leader.

13. Which of these is an antonym for 'upright' in the second paragraph?
    a. callous
    b. unprincipled
    c. horizontal
    d. collapsed

14. Which of these words is not an antonym for 'enduring'?
    a. fleeting
    b. brief
    c. short
    d. broad

15. Which word could replace 'regard' in the second paragraph?
    a. judge
    b. guess
    c. check
    d. criticise

16. 'Countless retellings' suggests
    a. people are bored with the story
    b. the story is fascinating
    c. people will lose interest eventually
    d. the stories are exaggerate

Read the extract and answer the questions that follow.

Gold has been a commodity highly prized throughout history. People have striven to accumulate it, have fashioned exquisite jewellery from it and have committed crimes to acquire it.

Deposits of gold in the earth form in two ways. Most are found in veins in rock, combined with quartz and other types of mineral such as silver. Most gold mining focuses on gold in veins like this. The open-cut mines are dug ever deeper as the gold close to the surface is exhausted. Recently, new gold mines to take advantage of gold close to the surface have been developed in Russia, Indonesia and Papua New Guinea, but there are strong concerns about possible harm to the environment.

Alluvial gold is created when dense grains from weathered rock wash down into the beds of streams and rivers. The gold is retrieved by panning, an operation in which water is scooped into a pan and swirled around until the heavier particles sink to the bottom and can be picked out. This is not done on any large scale anywhere.

Gold has always been used as currency. However, gold coins are heavy and difficult to carry in large quantities. Nowadays, gold is formed into bars and these make up a nation's gold reserves. The USA has the largest store of these and Germany is next in line.

Gold has been used in dentistry for many years for fillings or even for false teeth

as it resists corrosion. It is often mixed with various other metals – silver, copper or zinc – to make it stronger. Another use for gold is in electronic components because it is a good conductor of electricity. Annually, two hundred tons of gold are used world-wide in the electronics industry.

1. **What group of words could replace 'commodity' in the first sentence?**
   a. type of metal
   b. kind of currency
   c. article of trade
   d. material for jewellery

2. **The meaning of 'exhausted' in the second paragraph is**
   a. fatigued
   b. depleted
   c. processed
   d. discovered

3. **Which of these statements is true?**
   a. The bulk of gold mining is of alluvial gold.
   b. Every year, 200 tons of gold are used in dentistry.
   c. Gold is used in electronics because it resists corrosion.
   d. Gold coins have limited use in currency.

4. **Alluvial gold**
   a. may have the potential to harm the environment
   b. is heavier than gold found in veins in rock
   c. is not accessed commercially
   d. is accessed by open-cut mines

5. **The various excellent qualities of gold are described**
   a. in the third paragraph
   b. in the fourth paragraph
   c. in the fifth paragraph
   d. in the second paragraph

6. **Gold is used in dentistry**
   a. because it keeps its value
   b. because it looks good
   c. because it conducts electricity well
   d. because it is durable

7. **From the text, which of these conclusions can you draw?**
   a. Most people prefer to have gold fillings.
   b. Gold mining will continue.
   c. Gold currency will be used again in the future.
   d. More gold could be used in electronics.

8. **This text is**
   a. persuasive
   b. descriptive
   c. informative
   d. analytical

9. **The language of the text is**
   a. scientific vocabulary
   b. informal language
   c. technical language

10. **Which word can be substituted for 'components' in the last paragraph?**
    a. products
    b. elements
    c. gadgets
    d. designs

11. **'A good conductor of electricity' would**
    a. block the current
    b. prevent electric shocks
    c. not be affected by the current
    d. permit the passage of electricity

12. **Why might not panning be carried out now on a large scale?**
    a. The stores of alluvial gold have completely run out.
    b. There are concerns about harm to the environment.
    c. The technology is in the process of being upgraded.
    d. It requires too much labour and time.

13. **Which fact cannot be found in the text?**
    a. Gold reserves take the form of gold bars.
    b. The gold reserves are usually kept in capital cities.
    c. America has the largest store of gold reserves.
    d. Germany has the second largest store of gold reserves.

14. **Which of these might the text form part of?**
    a. an almanac
    b. a directory
    c. an article
    d. a chronicle

15. **'Weathered rock' in the third paragraph is**
    a. rock that has been affected by sun, wind and rain
    b. rock that is very unstable
    c. rock that is in gold mines
    d. rock that does not contain gold

Read the extract and answer the questions that follow.

The King of Vietnam owned a beautiful cat which he doted upon. It dined upon the finest delicacies and had a special servant whose job it was to brush the cat's fine grey fur. However, one of the King's officials coveted the cat and one day, seizing an opportunity, stole it and took it to his house.

In his house, the man whose name was Trang, set about training the cat. He placed two plates of food upon the floor. One was filled with pieces of the best fish, while the other contained only a small amount of food scraps. Trang positioned the cat between the two. Of course, the cat lunged towards the plate of fish, exactly the type of food it was expecting. What it was not expecting was that it should receive a sharp rap with a stick and be forcefully moved to the plate of scraps. Every time the cat veered towards the superior plate, it was thwarted. And thus the cat's training continued every day until it ignored the succulent fish and went directly to the garbage scraps.

The King learned where his cat was and sent his soldiers to bring both Trang and the cat to him. The King threatened his official with imprisonment or worse! Trang protested that his cat bore only a passing resemblance to the King's missing cat and offered to prove that the animal was, in fact, his own cat.

"Everyone knows that your cat is a real gourmet," he said, "and would never eat kitchen scraps. Let us put that to the test."

Two plates of food, different in quality and quantity, were set before the cat. Of course, the cat passed the test! Trang took the cat home, leaving the King very despondent.

---

1. **Which word is a synonym for 'doted'?**
   a. gazed
   b. accepted
   c. idolised
   d. honoured

2. **'Succulent fish' would be**
   a. plump fish
   b. tender fish
   c. various fish
   d. uncooked fish

3. **What might Trang's feelings have been after stealing the cat?**
   a. gratitude and nervousness
   b. remorse and anxiety
   c. satisfaction and anticipation
   d. delight and contentment

4. **If the cat was 'thwarted' it was**
   a. beaten
   b. dragged away
   c. frustrated
   d. starved

5. Trang said the cat 'bore only a passing resemblance' to the King's cat. This means
   a. Trang's cat was exactly like the king's cat in many ways
   b. no –one could really mistake one cat for the other
   c. the two cats resembled each other
   d. the cat looked different since it had been in Trang's possession

6. 'The cat passed the test.' This means
   a. the cat proved it was a gourmet
   b. the cat showed it had learned its lesson
   c. the cat showed it was afraid of Trang
   d. the cat displayed preference for Trang

7. What words could be used to describe Trang?
   a. shrewd and rash
   b. envious but just
   c. calculating and cruel
   d. foolish and sentimental

8. The King could have executed Trang for stealing the cat. This shows
   a. Trang was very foolish to steal the cat.
   b. The King had unlimited power.
   c. The King loved his cat very much.
   d. All of the above.

9. Into which category does the story fit?
   a. historical recount
   b. legend
   c. fantasy
   d. science fiction

10. 'Coveted' the cat means
   a. admired the cat
   b. was jealous of the cat's privileges
   c. was captivated by the cat's beauty
   d. longed to possess the cat

11. Trang trained the cat by
   a. repetition and cruelty
   b. kindness and example
   c. harshness and example
   d. repetition and commands

12. 'Thus' in the last sentence of the second paragraph means
   a. however
   b. consequently
   c. after this
   d. in this way

13. Trang's motive for stealing the cat was
   a. its beauty
   b. jealousy and greed
   c. arrogance
   d. a desire to show his own cleverness

14. If the King was despondent, he was
   a. frustrated
   b. downhearted
   c. furious
   d. disappointed

15. Which word is closest in meaning to a 'rap'?
   a. a pat
   b. a blow
   c. a caress
   d. a stroke

16. Which word could not be a synonym for 'ignored'?
   a. overlooked
   b. by-passed
   c. neglected
   d. focused

✪ UNIT 24   The Cockroach

Read the extract and answer the questions that follow.

The cockroach, a germ carrying insect pest, has been around for 300 million years and was scuttling about when the dinosaurs roamed the Earth. There are over 3500 different types of cockroaches; the bigger insects being found in hot countries and the smaller in cold countries.

The cockroach has a body encased in a hard shell; six, long, thin, hairy legs ending in small claws; two pairs of wings and two long, waving feelers which sense air movements signifying danger.

The cockroach lays its eggs in little sacs, called purses, which prevent the eggs drying out before they hatch. Some species carry the eggs about with them until this happens, usually in about eight weeks. The wingless baby cockroaches, called nymphs, moult several times as they grow, sometimes as frequently as once a week.

The cockroach eats absolutely anything – dead plants and animals, food, even wood! It likes a warm place to live and cannot survive in cold places. This nocturnal insect lives for months or years, depending on the species. It can survive for up to a month without water, and up to three months without food. It has been recorded that a cockroach was observed to live for a month without a head!

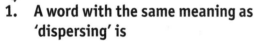

The cockroach spreads germs because it crawls over food, shedding bits of its body and dispersing bacteria. On the good side, this insect helps to dispose of dead plants and animals, and its droppings mix with the soil, helping to improve it. As well, it forms part of the food chain, as lizards, frogs and even people eat them.

1. **A word with the same meaning as 'dispersing' is**
    a. collecting
    b. scattering
    c. growing
    d. attracting

2. **An antonym for 'scuttling' would be**
    a. scampering
    b. darting
    c. ambling
    d. gamboling

3. **The cockroach's body is**
    a. rigid
    b. elongated
    c. hairy
    d. shiny

4. **The main topic of the third paragraph is**
    a. appearance
    b. habitat
    c. distribution
    d. reproduction

5. In the third paragraph, what does 'this' refer to?
   a. the purse
   b. the cockroach
   c. the egg
   d. the hatching

6. Which of these is most dangerous to a cockroach?
   a. accumulating bacteria
   b. descending temperature
   c. lack of food
   d. inadequate moisture

7. Tick all of the statements which are true.
   a. [ ] There are 300 different species of cockroaches.
   b. [ ] Baby cockroaches are called 'nymphs'.
   c. [ ] All nymphs moult every week.
   d. [ ] Large cockroaches are found in cold countries.
   e. [ ] The feelers are sensitive to air being moved about.
   f. [ ] Cockroaches are preyed on by dogs and foxes.
   g. [ ] All cockroaches carry their eggs about with them.
   h. [ ] Some cockroaches live for years.
   i. [ ] Cockroaches can eat timber.
   j. [ ] Cockroaches seem to be almost indestructible.

8. "This nocturnal insect lives for months or years, depending on the species." This is an example of
   a. a complex sentence
   b. descriptive language
   c. technical language
   d. scientific data

9. This text could be found in which of these books?
   a. The Homeowner's Manual of Pest Control.
   b. Common Household Insects.
   c. Strange Things People Eat.
   d. Keeping Cockroaches as Pets.

10. The cockroach spreads disease
    a. with its saliva
    b. by casting off fragments of its body
    c. by biting
    d. by vomiting on food

11. 'A germ-carrying insect pest' is an example of
    a. a clause
    b. an adverbial phrase
    c. an opinion
    d. a noun group

12. Which statement about cockroaches is false?
    a. Young cockroaches grow new skins frequently.
    b. Cockroach droppings enhance soil quality.
    c. Cockroaches can exist in all climatic conditions.
    d. Cockroaches have two sets of wings.

13. Which paragraph details the insect's almost complete invulnerability?
    a. fifth
    b. second
    c. third
    d. fourth

14. Which of these words is not an antonym for 'frequently'?
    a. uncommonly
    b. expectedly
    c. occasionally
    d. irregularly

Read the menu and answer the questions that follow.

MEDIEVAL BANQUET

First course:

Elus Bakynin Dyshes (eels baked in red wine)
Henne in Bokenade (chicken stewed in broth and herbs)
Chyces (roasted chickpeas boiled in garlic and wine)
Salmon (poached in beer)

Second Course:

Pourcelot Farci (roast pig stuffed with egg yolks, cheese and nuts)
Venyson Bake (venison pie with eggs, honey and spices)
Stewed Beeff (beef ribs baked in wine, with currants and onions)
Torta Inivre (a chicken pie topped with sugar and rosewater)
A Dauce Egre (fish in sweet and sour sauce)
Perry of Pesoun (a dish of cooked peas)
Salat (a salad of carrot and shrimp)
Pandemayne (fine white bread)
The finest French wine

Third Course:

Apple Muse (apples, almond milk and honey)
Sambrocade (elderflower cheesecake)
Bryndons (small cakes in a sauce of wine, fruit and nuts)
Gyngerbrede (a sweet honey candy)
Clarry (hot wine with honey and spices)

1. **How many different methods of cooking are there?**
   a. three
   b. four
   c. five
   d. six

2. **How many dishes contain vegetables?**
   a. three
   b. four
   c. five
   d. six

3. **How many fish dishes are there?**
   a. two
   b. three
   c. four
   d. five

4. **The dish of chickpeas is called**
   a. Salat
   b. Clarry
   c. Pandemayne
   d. Chyces

5. **The Medieval name of the elderflower cheesecake is**
   a. Gyngerbrede
   b. Sambrocade
   c. Perry of Pouson
   d. Bryndons

6. **How many dishes are cooked with wine?**
   a. one
   b. two
   c. three
   d. four

7. **How many dishes contain nuts?**
   a. one
   b. two
   c. three
   d. four

8. **Torta Inivre contains**
   a. beef
   b. chicken
   c. venison
   d. fish

9. **The hot wine drink is called**
   a. Perry
   b. Cherry
   c. Apple Muse
   d. Clarry

10. **Small cakes in a sauce are called**
    a. Gyngerbrede
    b. Pourcelot Farci
    c. Pandemayne
    d. Bryndons

11. **The main ingredient of A Dauce Egre is**
    a. goose
    b. hare
    c. fish
    d. eels

12. **From the menu, it seems that the medieval diet was lacking in**
    a. meat
    b. vegetables and fruit
    c. sweetening
    d. variety

13. **Whom do you think might have had this type of meal?**
    a. farm workers
    b. rich people
    c. everyone
    d. city people

14. **Honey as a sweetener is used in how many dishes?**
    a. one
    b. two
    c. three
    d. four

15. **A Dauce Egre is**
    a. a chicken dish
    b. a concoction of chickpeas
    c. fine white bread
    d. a fish course

16. **How many dishes are poached as a cooking method?**
    a. one
    b. two
    c. three
    d. none

17. **17. Tick all of the statements which are true.**
    a. [ ] Perry of Pouson contains pears.
    b. [ ] There are two chicken courses.
    c. [ ] There is a salad of crab and shrimp.
    d. [ ] The salmon is poached in wine.
    e. [ ] There are two pies on the menu.
    f. [ ] Two of the second course dishes have wine as an ingredient.
    g. [ ] Apple Muse contains almond milk.
    h. [ ] Clarry is served hot.

18. **Which of these means the same as 'Medieval'?**
    a. Ancient History
    b. Prehistory
    c. Middle Ages
    d. the Modern Age

Read the extract and answer the questions that follow.

The Sun, the only star in our Solar System, is 150 million kilometres from Earth. With a diameter of 1 392 000 kilometres, it has a mass which is 333 000 times greater than that of the Earth. Without the Sun, life would not exist on Earth. Our planet falls within what is known as the 'Life Zone'. A planet needs to be the right distance from the Sun for life to develop; between 120 million and 240 million kilometres is the crucial figure.

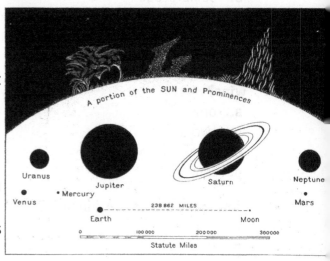

If the Sun were hotter, it would not have its characteristic golden hue – it would be blue or white. If it were cooler, it would glow red. Particles of matter (a million tons every second) are thrown off by the Sun and whirl away in all directions. These particles travel as far as the Earth and beyond. They are repelled by the magnetism of the Earth, except for the area around the Poles. Here, they enter the atmosphere and cause the spectacular glimmering colours known as the aurora or the Northern Lights.

Storms roil across the surface of the Sun. These sometimes propel vast amounts of gas into space. If this gas moves close enough to Earth, it can cause problems for us: power cuts and disruptions in mobile phone coverage.

Eventually, the Sun will stop providing life-giving heat and will collapse upon itself, becoming what is known as a Red Giant. The next stage of its destruction will be that the gas on the exterior drifts away, leaving a small star known as a White Dwarf. The good news for us is that this will not happen for about five billion years!

1. **A word that could be substituted for 'characteristic' in the first sentence of the second paragraph is**
   a. quality
   b. distinguishing
   c. constant
   d. radiant

2. **An antonym for 'repelled' is**
   a. deterred
   b. maintained
   c. invited
   d. propelled

3. **What is 'the crucial figure'?**
   a. 120 million km
   b. the right distance from the Sun
   c. between 120 million and 240 million km
   d. 240 million km

4. **The Northern Lights are caused by**
   a. gas from the Sun
   b. the repulsion of the Earth's magnetism
   c. solar storms
   d. particles of matter shed by the Sun

5. **If the Sun were cooler it would be**
   a. A Red Giant
   b. red
   c. blue
   d. a White Dwarf

6. **"Even though the Sun is so far distant, it can affect our daily lives on Earth." To which paragraph could this sentence be added as a concluding sentence?**
   a. first
   b. second
   c. third
   d. fourth

7. **Which sequence of steps describes the destruction of the Sun?**
   a. The gas drifts away. The Sun becomes a Red Giant. It collapses. It becomes a White Dwarf.
   b. The Sun collapses. It becomes a White Dwarf. The gas drifts away. It becomes a Red Giant.
   c. The Sun becomes a Red Giant. It collapses. The gas drifts away. It becomes a White Dwarf.
   d. The Sun collapses. It becomes a Red Giant. The gas drifts away. It becomes a White Dwarf.

8. **"Storms roil across the surface of the Sun." This suggests that the storms are**
   a. infrequent
   b. tumultuous
   c. short-lived
   d. insignificant

9. **Which of these statements is true?**
   a. The 'Life Zone' is less than 120 million kilometres from the Sun.
   b. Particles of matter from the Sun cause disruptions in mobile phone coverage.
   c. A collapsed star is known as a White Dwarf.
   d. A million tons of matter fly off the Sun every second.

10. **The particles of matter thrown off by the Sun**
    a. are attracted to Earth
    b. glow red
    c. are dispersed throughout space
    d. are the product of storms on the Sun

11. **'These sometimes propel vast amounts of gas into space.' Which sentence conveys exactly the same information?**
    a. Solar storms invariably project huge amounts of gas into space.
    b. Solar storms do not always produce gas clouds.
    c. Solar storms never vary in the amount of gas they project into space.
    d. Large amounts of gas are occasionally projected into space by solar storms.

12. **'In all directions' is an example of**
    a. a clause
    b. an adverbial phrase
    c. a metaphor
    d. a noun group

13. **This text can be classified as**
    a. an explanation
    b. a description
    c. an information report
    d. a commentary

Read the letters and answer the questions that follow.

Dear Sir,

I am a regular patron of Ellenborough's excellent public library. The range of material and the efficiency of the services provided is the equal of any library in a larger city. However, I wish to draw your attention and that of your readers to a relatively new and very worrying phenomenon. Many homeless people are creeping in and occupying the public reading areas for many hours each day. They don't read – they just occupy the chairs. They are all extremely dirty and they SMELL! Last week, I had a most upsetting experience. Upon entering the Ladies' Toilet, I found one of these people had washed her hair and was drying it under the hot-air blower! When I remonstrated with her, she told me it was none of my business. As a rate payer and a long-term user of the library, I most certainly is my business.

My attempts to alert the library administration to the seriousness of the problem have met a brick wall. Their view is that these people have equal rights to use the library. But, surely, they could insist that they wash themselves and put on clean clothes before they come in!

Concerned Library User, Bascott

Dear Sir,

I am one of the homeless people who find welcome refuge from the bitter Winter weather in the public library. I read Concerned Library User's letter with sadness rather than anger as she clearly has no idea how life is for other people.

Madam, you are being rather illogical. You complain that we smell and that you wish we would wash before coming in. Yet, you were appalled when one of our number attempted to wash her hair in the Ladies!

No doubt, Madam, you are amazed that I read the newspaper and that I am replying to you in a semi-literate fashion. We were not always homeless and you might be surprised to discover the background of some of 'these people' you refer to with such disdain.

I think I can speak for my vagabond comrades when I say how grateful we are for the warmth and comfort offered by the library and for the way we are treated just as ordinary people.

Harry, No Fixed Address

1. **If Concerned Library User 'remonstrated' with the homeless woman, she**
   a. tried to stop the woman using the hot-air blower
   b. complained to the woman that she didn't like her behaviour
   c. threatened to call the library staff
   d. argued very forcibly with the woman

2. **Why does the first letter writer put SMELL all in capital letters?**
   a. To encourage them to wash in the toilet facilities.
   b. To reveal her extreme disgust at the homeless people.
   c. To display her frustration with the library administration.
   d. Because she wants to use the public reading areas.

3. **Which of these statements is true?**
   a. Harry always washes his hair in the Men's toilet facilities.
   b. The library staff asked the homeless people to wash.
   c. Ellensborough is a small city.
   d. Ellensborough has no facilities for homeless people.

4. **The first letter writer's use of the expression 'these people' reveals**
   a. frustration
   b. bias
   c. lack of imagination
   d. foolishness

5. **Concerned Letter Writer feels she has the right to complain because she is**
   a. concerned and perturbed
   b. upset by the homeless people's behaviour
   c. a rate payer and library patron
   d. disgusted by the way the homeless people smell

6. **'Have met a brick wall' is an example of**
   a. a simile
   b. an opinion
   c. hyperbole
   d. a metaphor

7. **How would you describe the writer of the second letter?**
   a. illiterate
   b. semi-literate
   c. somewhat literate
   d. highly literate

8. **A synonym for 'disdain' is**
   a. impoliteness
   b. anger
   c. inexactness
   d. condescension

9. **Which of these phrases has a similar meaning to 'my vagabond comrades'?**
   a. like-thinking people
   b. people wandering the streets
   c. regular library users
   d. brothers in arms

10. **'One of our number' means**
    a. there are a number of homeless people
    b. there are too many homeless people to count
    c. a member of the homeless people in the library
    d. one single person

11. **Homeless people have as much right as anyone else to use the library. Whose view is this?**
    a. Harry and his friends
    b. the library administration
    c. the editor
    d. the newspaper's readers

12. **Why does Harry describe himself as of 'No Fixed Address'?**
    a. To make the first letter writer feel bad?
    b. To enlist the reader's sympathies.
    c. To show his shame at being homeless.
    d. To emphasise his homeless status.

13. **To whom is the first letter addressed?**
    a. the homeless people
    b. the editor
    c. the editor and the readers
    d. the library administration

14. **To whom is the second letter addressed?**
    a. the library administration
    b. the editor and readers
    c. the first letter writer
    d. the first letter writer, the editor and the readers

Read and complete the cloze passage with words from the that follow.

The story of the famed Swiss folk hero, William Tell, was first written down in the 15th century. He was _____ for his strength and his excellent marksmanship with the crossbow. During his _____, Switzerland was under the hated _____ of Austria. The Austrian official in charge of Tell's village had placed his cap upon a pole and all people were _____ to bow to it. One day, when with his young son, Tell refused to bow. He was immediately arrested and both he and his little boy were told they would be executed. However, Tell could win a _____ by shooting an arrow from his son's head with one clean shot. Tell succeeded and won their _____ . But, the official had noticed that Tell had removed two arrows from his quiver, _____ to shooting. When questioned, Tell said that if he had _____ killed his son, the next arrow would have been for the official!

1. a. derided
    b. renounced
    c. rebuked
    d. renowned

2. a. chronicle
    b. leadership
    c. lifetime
    d. history

3. a. observation
    b. alliance
    c. imprisonment
    d. control

4. a. elated
    b. obliged
    c. forbidden
    d. gratified

5. a. prize
    b. reprieve
    c. wager
    d. honour

6. a. debate
    b. accomplishment
    c. liberty
    d. containment

7. a. prior
    b. further
    c. subsequent
    d. simultaneous

8. a. intentionally
    b. accidentally
    c. viciously
    d. heedlessly

9. Tell was a 'folk hero'. This suggests that
   a. the tale is based on fact
   b. the story may not be completely true
   c. the story was never written down
   d. the story is a total fantasy

10. Tell was renowned for
    a. his opposition to Austrian rule
    b. his fighting ability and physical strength
    c. his archery skills and bodily strength
    d. his physical size and skill with the bow

11. Switzerland was under the _____ of Austria.
    a. benevolence
    b. assistance
    c. recommendation
    d. domination

12. Tell's act of rebellion was due to
    a. humour
    b. dissatisfaction
    c. pride
    d. strength

13. 'One clean shot' means
    a. one rapid shot
    b. one slow. careful shot
    c. the best shot of a number
    d. one attempt

14. If Tell failed in his test, his intention was
    a. to flee
    b. to kill the Austrian governor
    c. to kill the officer in charge
    d. to enlist the help of the townspeople

15. Bowing to the cap was intended to be a sign of
    a. submission
    b. fondness
    c. admiration
    d. good sense

16. A synonym for 'renowned' is
    a. a. criticised
    b. compensated
    c. assessed
    d. celebrated

17. If people were 'obliged to', they were
    a. resigned to
    b. required to
    c. reputed to
    d. provoked to

18. The story of William Tell is
    a. accurate
    b. instructive
    c. bizarre
    d. legendary

19. A synonym for 'reprieve' is
    a. committal
    b. acquittal
    c. reward
    d. reputation

20. An antonym for 'prior' is
    a. previous
    b. simultaneous
    c. preparatory
    d. subsequent

21. This story would most likely to be found in which of these?
    a. 'Ancient Heroes.'
    b. 'Archery Skills.'
    c. 'Inspiring Legends.'
    d. 'Modern Stories of Daring and Courage.'

Read the extract and answer the questions that follow.

The idea of a new beginning or being able to make a fresh start is an attractive concept for all people. In Australian culture, New Year's Day provides the opportunity to make resolutions to turn over a new leaf and to get our lives in order. In India, this opportunity is provided by Diwali, the Hindu festival of lights. Hindus believe that light (goodness) triumphs over darkness (evil), providing a time full of promise.

Diwali (a contraction of Deepavali – a row of lights) is held during October or November. Lights appear everywhere – in temples and in streets, festooning trees and decorating doors and windows of houses.

As the time for the festival draws near, an air of anticipation develops. People prepare for Diwali by thoroughly cleaning their houses and sometimes repainting them. They create intricate red and yellow Rangoli patterns on the floors of their houses and on the pavements outside. The red and yellow colour is meant to intimidate evil spirits, ensuring that the days of the festival are auspicious.

On the first day of the five day festival, each household buys and lights a new and special clay lamp to symbolise a new beginning. Everyone bathes and puts on new clothes. Women wear their best jewellery and paint delicate patterns with henna on their hands and feet. After praying at their household shrine, they go visiting family and friends, taking gifts. Each night there is dancing and fire crackers explode for four or five hours, culminating in huge displays on the last night in major towns and cities.

1. **'To turn over a new leaf' is an example of**
   a. a simile
   b. a clause
   c. a pun
   d. a metaphor

2. **A word which could replace 'resolutions' is**
   a. answers
   b. undertakings
   c. opportunities
   d. scripts

3. **Why is information included in brackets in the first sentence of the second paragraph?**
   a. To show the correct spelling of Diwali.
   b. To explain the name of the festival.
   c. To instruct in the pronunciation of the name.
   d. To reveal the history of Diwali.

4. **'Light triumphs over darkness'. The darkness symbolises**
   a. night
   b. uncleanness
   c. evil
   d. our old lives

5. **'An air of anticipation develops.' The sentence which has most nearly the same meaning is**
   a. People know they must prepare painstakingly for Diwali.
   b. People enjoy themselves thoroughly during the festival.
   c. As Diwali approaches, people become very anxious.
   d. People eagerly wait for the festival to start.

6. **The outward symbol of a new beginning at this time is**
   a. new clothes for everyone
   b. Rangoli patterns
   c. a new lamp
   d. cleaning and repainting houses

7. **Which of these words is an antonym for 'auspicious'?**
   a. appropriate
   b. promising
   c. blessed
   d. ominous

8. **Which of these sentences contain information that can be found in the text?**
   a. [   ] Diwali lasts five days.
   b. [   ] Outside India, Diwali is celebrated more simply.
   c. [   ] Red and yellow are thought to frighten evil spirits away.
   d. [   ] Special food is prepared and eaten during Diwali.
   e. [   ] Spectacular fireworks displays take place on the last night.
   f. [   ] People pray to the goddess Lakshmi at this time.
   g. [   ] Fireworks are intended to drive away evil spirits.
   h. [   ] People share hospitality at this time.

9. **'Festooning trees' is**
   a. covering trees
   b. adorning trees
   c. illuminating trees
   d. obscuring trees

10. **'To turn' is**
    a. a finite verb
    b. a non-finite verb
    c. a participle
    d. a verb group

11. **Which of these statements is true?**
    a. Red and yellow clothes are worn during Diwali.
    b. Diwali starts on the same day as New Year.
    c. Diwali is on the same days each year.
    d. Diwali is regarded as full of promise.

12. **The text suggests that**
    a. Diwali is commercialised.
    b. Diwali fills people with optimism.
    c. Not everyone participates in Diwali.
    d. Diwali is going out of fashion.

13. **The last sentence of the fourth paragraph is**
    a. a complex sentence
    b. a simple sentence
    c. a compound sentence
    d. an expression of opinion

14. **Which of these words has a similar meaning to 'intimidate'?**
    a. daunt
    b. reassure
    c. engage
    d. collaborate

Read the extract and answer the questions that follow.

Louis XVI of France was an interesting person. During his long reign of seventy-two years, he led the country to become a major power in Europe, but his excessively luxurious lifestyle irked his subjects.

Louis ordered the huge and opulent Palace of Versailles to be built. It was a massive construction undertaking and at one time, 36 000 people were working on it. The gardens contain 1400 fountains. Louis attempted to conceal this extravagance by permitting only minimal operation of the fountains and by forbidding anyone to mention them!

Louis had an aversion to washing and only took three baths in his entire lifetime! He thought it only necessary to wash the tip of his nose. The courtiers were obliged to copy him, so they, too, only washed the tips of their noses and claimed to have given up all other bathing.

Louis did like his food – and plenty of it! A typical lunch for him might include four bowls of soup to begin, followed by two whole chickens, ham, lamb, beef, fish, salad and eggs, and concluded with cakes and fruit. Louis had been told that champagne was good for him, so lunch (and dinner) was always accompanied by copious quantities of it. When Louis died, the doctors examining his body declared that his stomach was twice the normal size.

Louis had another peculiarity, too. He had problems sleeping so he had four hundred and thirteen beds and moved from one to another all night. Perhaps, indigestion kept him awake?

---

1. **A word with a similar meaning to 'irked' is**
   a. amused
   b. delighted
   c. dumbfounded
   d. displeased

2. **The first paragraph suggests that Louis was**
   a. a real buffoon
   b. a clever statesman
   c. a lazy monarch
   d. a gourmet

3. **What did Louis wish to keep hidden from the public?**
   a. The number of people working on Versailles.
   b. His unhygienic personal habits.
   c. The excessiveness of aspects of Versailles.
   d. The lavishness of his daily diet.

4. **The phrase which has most nearly the same meaning as 'an aversion to washing' is**
   a. an allergy to washing
   b. a great dislike of washing
   c. no reason to wash
   d. no facilities for washing

5. **The word 'claimed' in the third paragraph suggests that**
   a. the courtiers were proud not to wash
   b. the courtiers were delighted not to have to wash
   c. the courtiers objected to being forbidden to wash
   d. the courtiers probably pretended not to wash

6. **Louis' dining habits were**
   a. exemplary
   b. gluttonous
   c. exaggerated
   d. prudent

7. **Which of these statements is true?**
   a. The fountains were constantly in use.
   b. Louis had 413 rooms in his palace.
   c. Louis was a moderate consumer of champagne.
   d. Louis' food intake caused bodily changes.

8. **What is the purpose of the last sentence?**
   a. To explain the reasons for Louis' insomnia.
   b. To conclude the paragraph.
   c. To express a negative opinion of Louis' diet.
   d. To make the reader think more about the subject.

9. **Which word could replace 'peculiarity' in the last paragraph?**
   a. familiarity
   b. eccentricity
   c. habit
   d. maxim

10. **Which of these facts cannot be found in the text?**
    a. Louis began lunch with four bowls of soup.
    b. The main courses included beef, lamb, veal and chicken.
    c. Louis enjoyed champagne with his meals.
    d. Louis consumed fruit desserts and cakes.

11. **A synonym for 'copious' is**
    a. meagre
    b. adequate
    c. bountiful
    d. tolerable

12. **An antonym for 'opulent' could be**
    a. sumptuous
    b. extensive
    c. well-furnished
    d. impoverished

13. **In which of these books might you find this text?**
    a. 'Spinechilling Mysteries.'
    b. 'Strange But True.'
    c. 'Travellers' Atlas for France.'
    d. 'Mythical Monarchs.'

Read the extract and answer the questions that follow.

The most gargantuan of all dinosaurs, the Sauropods, a species of the "lizard-hipped" dinosaurs, were the largest animals ever to have lived on land. They first appeared during the late Triassic Period, became prolific in the Late Jurassic Period, and died out in the Late Cretaceous Period. Fossilised remains have been discovered all around the world except for Antarctica. A large specimen uncovered in Queensland and dubbed "Eliot" after the farmer who discovered it, had a thigh-bone measuring 1.6 metres, leading to the conclusion that it may have been 21 metres in length and weighed 30 tons. However, footprints of a sauropod found in Western Australia were 1.7 metres across, prompting speculation that this dinosaur could have been 45 metres long!

    Within the classification of Sauropoda, there were several types of dinosaur: diplodocids, brachiosaurids and titanosaurs. They varied slightly within the same overall body shape. Diplodocids were very long with even longer tails. Brachiosaurids were tall and titanosaurs could have massive, bulky bodies. However, all were herbivorous quadrupeds that travelled about in herds. They had either spatulate teeth (narrow at the gums and broadening out) or peg-shaped teeth, both designed to efficiently grind up the huge amount of vegetation they needed to consume each day to sustain life. It has been ascertained by scientists that they swallowed stones which stayed in their stomachs as a further digestive aid.

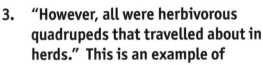

    Footprints of sauropods have shown that when they travelled, it was either in single file, with the young ones placed at the front of the line or in two parallel lines. It was once thought that these dinosaurs could stand upright, using their tails as an aid to balance, but this theory has now been discredited.

1. **'Prolific' in the second sentence has a similar meaning to**
   a. meagre
   b. teeming
   c. inexhaustible
   d. dominant

2. **'Speculation' means**
   a. scientific research
   b. data
   c. fantasies
   d. hypotheses

3. **"However, all were herbivorous quadrupeds that travelled about in herds." This is an example of**
   a. the writer's supposition
   b. an unfounded generalisation
   c. technical language
   d. a scientist's theory

4. **Elliot's thigh bone supports the contention that this dinosaur may have weighed**
   a. 21 tons
   b. 45 tons
   c. 30 tons
   d. 16 tons

5. **All sauropods**
   a. had spatulate teeth
   b. had very long tails
   c. could walk on two legs
   d. were lizard hipped

6. **"They varied slightly within the same overall body shape". The sentence which best expresses this idea is**
   a. The similarities between sauropods were outweighed by the differences.
   b. The various types of sauropods did not resemble each other.
   c. The variations in shape were less important than the similarities.
   d. The different types of sauropods were impossible to tell apart.

7. **The text suggests that the sauropods' diet**
   a. was monotonous
   b. was nutritious
   c. was difficult to digest
   d. was inadequate

8. **Which of these statements is true?**
   a. The longest sauropod thigh-bone was found in Western Australia.
   b. Sauropods lived a solitary existence.
   c. Brachiosaurids had exceptionally long tails.
   d. Sauropods could not function as bipeds.

9. **From the text, what conclusion can you draw about sauropod research?**
   a. It has been concluded
   b. It is a continuous process.
   c. It is inadequate.
   d. It is vitally important.

10. **According to the text, sauropods**
    a. were omnivorous
    b. existed in all continents
    c. died out during the Triassic Period
    d. were the most considerable in bulk of all dinosaurs

11. **'Ascertained' means**
    a. refuted
    b. determined
    c. queried
    d. pondered

12. **Which of these theories has been discredited?**
    a. Sauropods used stones as a digestive aid.
    b. Sauropods always travelled in single file.
    c. Sauropods could maintain an upright stance.
    d. Sauropods possibly weighed more than 30 tons.

13. **Which of these could not be an antonym for 'discredited'?**
    a. verified
    b. upheld
    c. supported
    d. overwhelmed

14. **'Fossilised remains' is an example of**
    a. a noun group
    b. a verb group
    c. an adjectival phrase
    d. slang

Read the extract and answer the questions that follow.

Once there lived a poor widow who had a small son called Paddy. Like many small boys, Paddy disliked stopping his playtime and going to bed at night. His mother would suggest, and then request that he go to bed, but it was not until her lips set in a firm line that he would reluctantly go to his little box bed in the room next to the kitchen.

One night, his mother was extremely tired and she went to bed, saying, "Stay if you will, Paddy, but if the old fairy-wife comes to take you away, it will be your own fault for disobeying me."

Paddy continued his play, but suddenly there was a scuffling in the chimney and a house-brownie jumped into the room. (House-brownies loved to clean up people's houses, leaving them spick and span. Usually the house-owners left out treats such as oatcakes or cups of goats' cream as payment.)

"What's your name?" asked Paddy of the small, skinny-legged, large-eyed creature.

"It's Ainsel (own self)," replied the brownie. "What's yours?"

But, Paddy could be clever, too and he said, "My Ainsel."

The brownie and the boy played some lively games. Then, Paddy stirred up the fire as the room was growing cold and a cinder fell out onto Ainsel's foot. Immediately, he began to shriek and wail. Upon this, a fierce voice shouted down the chimney. "Who has hurt you? I will come down the chimney and take them away!" (This was the old fairy-wife, who was the brownie's mother.)

"It was My Ainsel," sniffled the brownie.

"Then why are you making such a din if it was your own fault? Stop your sniveling." And with that, a long arm came down the chimney and whisked the brownie away. Paddy jumped up and ran to his bed, pulling his covers right over his head.

In the morning, Paddy's mother was surprised to find that not only was her house still in some disarray, but the treats, that she had left out for the brownie, were still untouched. However, she was delighted to discover that Paddy no longer made a fuss about going to bed, but took himself there the moment she suggested it.

1. **Which of these words is not a synonym for 'snivelling'?**
   a. blubbing
   b. brawling
   c. lamenting
   d. whimpering

2. **What is suggested by 'her lips set in a firm line'?**
   a. She had finished speaking
   b. She was getting angry.
   c. She was trying not to laugh
   d. She was very tired.

3. **'Spick and span' is an example of**
   a. onomatopoeia
   b. a simile
   c. a pun
   d. alliteration

4. **What is 'this' in the sentence 'Upon this...?**
   a. the brownie's foot
   b. the cinder falling out
   c. the brownie's cries
   d. the fairy-wife's reply

5. **The text suggests that the fairy-wife**
   a. is not concerned with Ainsel's problems
   b. is very strong
   c. is fed up with Ainsel's complaints
   d. wants Ainsel to be tougher

6. **Which of these words is an antonym for 'disarray'?**
   a. orderliness
   b. confusion
   c. grime
   d. busyness

7. **Which of these statements cannot be inferred from the text?**
   a. The brownie liked restoring order to a messy house.
   b. The brownie enjoyed playing games.
   c. The fairy-wife was protective of her son.
   d. The brownie was very much smaller than Paddy.

8. **Why did Paddy pull the covers right over his head?**
   a. He was chilled as the room had grown colder.
   b. He was trying to hide in case the fairy-wife returned.
   c. He didn't want his mother to disturb him.
   d. He had learned his lesson about going to bed on time.

9. **Which of these messages does the story convey?**
   a. Be careful what you wish for, as you may get it.
   b. Go to bed when you are told.
   c. Do not trust the fairy folk as they may betray you.
   d. Quick thinking may save you in a threatening situation.

10. **The beginning of the story reveals that Paddy was**
    a. clever
    b. resourceful
    c. disobedient
    d. compliant

11. **The middle of the story reveals that Paddy was also**
    a. over the moon
    b. on the ball
    c. out to lunch
    d. in a tizz

12. **The end of the story reveals that Paddy was finally**
    a. gloomy
    b. content
    c. astonished
    d. chastened

13. **'A scuffling' is an example of**
    a. hyperbole
    b. metaphor
    c. personification
    d. onomatopoeia

14. **The text is intended to**
    a. teach a moral
    b. recount factual events
    c. create sympathy for the brownie
    d. warn about fairy folk

Read the extract and answer the questions that follow.

The Book of Kells, the finest surviving Medieval manuscript, embellished with vibrant illustrations and kept under glass in the library of the Trinity College in Dublin, is over a thousand years old. It was probably commenced in the 9th century by monks living in a community on Iona, a small island off the Scottish coast. Because of its name, it is assumed that part of the Book was written at the town of Kells in County Meath. It is likely that the Book was moved there because of the danger of Viking raids on Iona. These frequent occurrences resulted in death of monks and pillage of the monastery.

The Book was stolen from during the 11th century. Its covers were ripped off and the book was cast into a ditch. The Book was recovered, but the cover, which probably was embellished with gold and jewels, was not.

Yet another danger to the Book occurred after the English Civil War in the 17th century, when monasteries and their treasures were under threat of destruction by Roundhead forces. The Book was sent to Dublin for safe keeping. Trinity College has subsequently been its home, except for the occasional times when it has been taken on international tours.

The Book of Kells has 680 pages, of which only two lack some sort of decoration. Some pages are devoted entirely to illustration, some have only a line or two of text, but the majority of the pages have elaborate illuminated first letters for the text. The pages of the Book are vellum (calf-skin tanned to paper thinness). The vivid dyes used in the decoration were extracted from the various parts of plants – berries, leaves, roots and bark – and from insects, lichen and metals. Scholars have concluded from an exhaustive study of the decoration that a minimum of four artists were involved in the execution of this magnificent work of Irish art.

1. **The meaning of 'execution' in the last sentence is**
    a. killing
    b. design
    c. completion
    d. occupation

2. **A synonym for 'pillage' in the first paragraph is**
    a. reconstruction
    b. robbery
    c. occupation
    d. evacuation

3. **The Book was moved to Kells from Iona because of**
    a. danger from the Roundheads
    b. the possibility of theft
    c. the menace of invaders
    d. the death of the artists

4. **Which of these statements are facts and which are theories? Write F for 'fact' and T for 'theory'.**
   a. [ ] The Book was begun in the 9th century.
   b. [ ] Part of the Book was written in County Meath.
   c. [ ] The Book has 680 pages.
   d. [ ] The Book was moved from Iona because of Viking raids.
   e. [ ] The Book was stolen in the 11th century.
   f. [ ] The Book was taken to Dublin in the 17th century.
   g. [ ] At least four artists worked on the Book.
   h. [ ] The Book rarely leaves Trinity College.

5. **Which event happened third in this recount?**
   a. The Book was commenced in the 9th century.
   b. The Book was taken to Dublin for safekeeping.
   c. The Book was moved to Kells in County Meath.
   d. The Book was stolen and recovered.

6. **"Yet another danger..." The purpose of this phrase is**
   a. to introduce a different idea
   b. to supply a topic sentence for the paragraph
   c. to supply a summary for what has gone before
   d. to provide humour in the text

7. **"The Book of Kells is the finest surviving example of Medieval literature and thus needs to be kept secure." To which paragraph could this sentence be added?**
   a. the first
   b. the second
   c. the third
   d. the fourth

8. **How long has the Book been kept in Dublin?**
   a. one thousand years
   b. about four hundred years
   c. since the 11th century
   d. under two hundred years

9. **Which fact cannot be found in the text?**
   a. Some dyes were obtained from insects.
   b. The dyes were brilliant in colour.
   c. Some of the dyes were imported and hence expensive.
   d. Some dyes were extracted from lichen.

10. **'An exhaustive study' would be**
    a. a very tiring one for the scholars
    b. a very thorough study
    c. one that is wearying to read
    d. a very restricted study

11. **The last sentence of the fourth paragraph suggests that**
    a. No-one takes the scholars' conclusions seriously.
    b. Different styles of art suggest different artists.
    c. Four artists could not have supplied all the decoration.
    d. There will need to be more research done.

12. **The purpose of the brackets in the last paragraph is**
    a. make an aside to the reader
    b. to show that other materials were also used
    c. to provide a reason for using vellum
    d. to explain an unfamiliar word

Read the extract and answer the questions that follow.

In 1935, Cane Toads were introduced to Australia from Hawaii to control the cane beetles which were creating havoc in the Queensland sugar cane crops. After disposing of the beetle pests, the Cane Toads settled into their new environment, multiplied at an extraordinary rate and became pests themselves.

Cane Toads are able to acclimatise themselves to widely varying habitats. Although most plentiful in grasslands and bush, they are equally at home in sandy dunes or in swampy mangroves. They can tolerate temperatures which range from a chilly 5 degrees to a sweltering 50 degrees! As a result, Toads can now be found throughout Queensland, in the Northern Territory and in some parts of New South Wales.

Large bodied Cane Toads have dry skin covered in warts and may be red, brown, olive, yellow or grey in hue. On their pale bellies, a scattering of dark spots can be observed. Their bony heads have prominent ridges which join above their eyes. While their back feet have rubbery webbing between the toes, the front feet do not. A mature female can weigh up to one kilo in weight while her male counterpart is smaller.

Cane Toads could be described as omnivorous as the tadpoles consume various aquatic plants while adult Toads eat virtually everything: insects, snails, smaller frogs, household scraps and even small mammals.

Cane Toads produce venom which oozes from their parotoid glands (on either side of their heads). This poison can kill native animals or people's pets if they seize the Toads in their mouths. Although there have been fatalities overseas from eating Toads, so far there have been no deaths of humans in Australia. However, even touching a Toad can cause inflammation, severe pain and even temporary blindness.

1. **The implication of 'an extraordinary rate' is**
   a. moderately slowly
   b. extremely fast
   c. at a steady rate
   d. immediately

2. **The second paragraph suggests that**
   a. Cane Toads will be fairly easily contained.
   b. There is no real reason to worry about the spread of Cane Toads.
   c. Cane Toads will eventually spread right through most of Australia.
   d. Cane Toads' adapt well to different environments.

3. **"Cane Toads are able to acclimatise themselves to widely varying habitats." This is an example of**
   a. the writer's views
   b. a complex sentence
   c. descriptive language
   d. a topic sentence

4. **Cane Toads have now spread to**
   a. all of N.S.W., the N.T. and all of Qld.
   b. the N.T., some of N.S.W. and southern Qld.
   c. some of N.S.W., all of Qld. and the N.T.
   d. northern Qld., the N.T. and northern N.S.W.

5. **The spread of Cane Toads can be attributed to**
   a. abundant breeding and warm weather
   b. ability to adapt and abundant breeding
   c. favourable weather and good food
   d. abundant breeding and a variety of food

6. **According to the text, which of the following is correct?**
   a. The parotoid glands are on the Toad's back.
   b. Toads' feet all have rubbery webbing between the toes.
   c. Toads have scaly skin covered in warts.
   a. Male Toads are slighter than female Toads.

7. **"Given their ability to adapt, it is hard to see how the advance of Cane Toads can be halted." To which paragraph can this be added?**
   a. the first
   b. the second
   c. the fourth
   d. the fifth

8. **If the cane beetles were 'creating havoc', they were most likely**
   a. making nests
   b. spreading disease
   c. biting the workers
   d. ruining the crop

9. **Which of these is the Toads' preferred environment?**
   a. deserts
   b. grasslands
   c. rainforest
   d. mangroves

10. **Which part of the Toad is described as 'rubbery'?**
    a. the parotoid glands
    b. the fingers
    c. the head ridges
    d. the toe webbing

11. **"Her male counterpart" is**
    a. her mating partner
    b. any mature male Toad
    c. her particular ally
    d. her male offspring

12. **Which fact is not in the text?**
    a. Cane Toads can be various colours.
    b. Cane Toads attack small animals.
    c. Cane Toad venom can cause short-term blindness.
    d. Cane Toads sit upright.

13. **"Cane Toads produce venom which oozes from their parotoid glands." This is an example of**
    a. a compound sentence
    b. a metaphor
    c. technical language
    d. informal language

14. **The last paragraph suggests**
    a. No-one will die from Cane Toad venom in Australia.
    b. We really don't need to worry about Cane Toads.
    c. The Cane Toad menace has been exaggerated.
    d. Cane Toads are potentially very dangerous.

15. **This text is**
    a. a recount
    b. a description
    c. a report
    d. an exposition

Read the extract and answer the questions that follow.

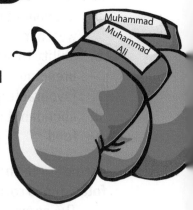

Muhammad Ali was born in 1942 with the name of Cassius Clay. At the age of twelve, he began to have boxing lessons and proved to be 'a natural' at this sport. At 17, he won the Golden Gloves title and a year later, added an Olympic gold medal.

Clay's self-confidence was supreme. "I am the greatest!" he told everyone. His belief in himself began to seem even more feasible when he became the heavy-weight champion of the world at the age of 22.

Shortly after this, Cassius Clay became a Muslim and took the name of Muhammad Ali. Although drafted into the US army to fight in the Vietnam War, he refused to go for religious reasons. The World Boxing Association was incensed with his stance and took away his title and forbade him to box in America. However, over time, their attitude mellowed and they rescinded their decision allowing him to box again.

In 1974, Muhammad Ali was once more champion of the world, by winning the heavy-weight crown. By now, his claim to be 'the greatest' did not seem to be an over-confident boast, but a true statement, and the world agreed with him. Yet, it seemed that something was wrong. He began to seem slower in the ring and his timing was sometimes off. At last, a diagnosis of Parkinson's Disease, a brain disease, was made.

Today, Muhammad Ali has trouble speaking and controlling his limbs, but he still works for charities and travels the world, speaking out for human rights. The courage which he displays in battling his condition and continuing to strive for justice and equality in the world, reveals that he is still 'the greatest'.

1. **If someone is 'incensed', they are**
   a. shocked
   b. displeased
   c. infuriated
   d. disbelieving

2. **A word similar in meaning to 'rescinded' is**
   a. affirmed
   b. authorised
   c. withdrew
   d. regretted

3. **Clay was 'a natural'. This means he**
   a. did not need boxing lessons
   b. boxed every day
   c. knew he was going to be great
   d. learned very quickly

4. **"Clay's self-confidence was supreme." This sentence which best expresses this idea is**
   a. Clay's self-assurance annoyed many people.
   b. Clay was simply boastful.
   c. Clay fully believed in his own potential.
   d. Clay was not more self-confident than other people.

5. The text suggests that the World Boxing Association took away his title because they thought he was
   a. deceitful
   b. not the greatest
   a. unpatriotic
   b. too boastful

6. What was 'his stance' in the third paragraph?
   a. his words
   b. his viewpoint
   c. his arrogance
   d. his performance

7. Which of these events happened first?
   a. He was stripped of his title.
   b. He became a Muslim.
   c. The World Boxing Association made a ruling.
   d. He was drafted for the Vietnam War.

8. Which of these statements is false?
   a. Muhammad Ali quickly revealed his potential as a fighter.
   b. He has not allowed his condition to stop his doing good works.
   c. Muhammad Ali won the heavy-weight title three times.
   d. He showed the first signs of greatness at age 22.

9. "This betrayal by his body must have been a bitter blow." To which paragraph could this sentence be added?
   a. first
   b. second
   c. third
   d. fourth

10. What is the writer's attitude towards Muhammad Ali?
    a. unbiased
    b. favourable
    c. defensive
    d. sceptical

11. 11. A 'feasible' belief is
    a. an irritating one
    b. a reasonable one
    c. one others don't agree with
    d. one worth imitating

12. The last sentence of the second paragraph is
    a. a simple sentence and a phrase
    b. a simple sentence
    c. a complex sentence
    d. a compound sentence

13. 'At last' is
    a. an adjectival phrase
    b. an adverbial phrase
    c. a participle phrase
    d. a noun phrase

14. Why is Ali still 'the Greatest'?
    a. No-one has ever equalled his exploits in the boxing ring.
    b. He travels constantly, despite his illness.
    c. Despite his disability, he is still a fighter for justice.
    d. He achieved what he set out to do.

15. Which of these books might this text form part of?
    a. 'A History of the World Boxing Association.'
    b. 'Modern Day Heroes.'
    c. 'Great Athletes of the Twenty-First Century.'
    d. 'Boxing for Fitness.'

✪ UNIT 36   Early Submarines

Read the extract and answer the questions that follow.

Inventors have been working on submarines or submersibles since the 17th century. A submarine is a vessel carrying a crew (even of only one person) which can submerge and travel independently. 'Submersible' is the term used for a similar crewed vessel capable of submerging and moving, but not necessarily under its own power.

    The first recorded submarine (or possibly submersible), the Drebbel, was designed by an Englishman, William Bourne, and built by a Dutchman, Cornelius Drebbel, who was in the service of England. The vessel was rowed with oars and trialed in 1630. It may have been towed behind a boat, but this is now impossible to verify.

    The first submarine attack in wartime was during the American War of Independence. The Turtle carried a mine which was hoped could be drilled into the wooden hull of the HMS Eagle. However, the hull of the ship was encased in an impenetrable metal plate and could not be breached. The Turtle slipped away.

    Until 1879, all submarines, whether moved by oars or by propellers were powered by the crew's muscle and their speed and usefulness were limited by this. An Englishman, the Reverend William Garnett, put a steam engine into his submarine. Even though this was a huge advance, the British Admiralty was not interested. Although Garnett teamed up with a Swedish businessman and built vessels for Germany, Turkey and Greece, the vessels did not ultimately prove successful and the inventor died destitute.

1. **The meaning of 'destitute' is**
   a. friendless
   b. prematurely
   c. penniless
   d. embittered

2. **The hull 'could not be breached' means?**
   a. could not be reached
   b. could not be split
   c. could not be seen
   d. could not be attached

3. **What is the purpose of the brackets in the second paragraph?**
   a. to add extra data
   b. to give another term for these vessels
   c. to cast doubt on whether it was actually a submarine
   d. because the author does not think it was really a submersible

4. **What is the main difference between a submarine and a submersible?**
   a. its size
   b. how many crew it carries
   c. speed of movement
   d. independence of movement

5. **The attack on the Eagle could best be described as**
   a. an unqualified success
   b. a fiasco
   c. a qualified success
   d. an expensive experiment

6. **Which of these statements is false?**
   a. The first steam powered submarines appeared after 1879.
   b. Submarines were in use during the American War of Independence.
   c. Cornelius Drebbel built the first recorded submarine.
   d. The Drebbel was designed by William Garnett.

7. **Which of these sentences best matches the ideas expressed in the first sentence of the last paragraph?**
   a. Before 1879, no-one had thought of putting engines into submarines.
   b. Submarines would not be able to move fast enough without some sort of engine.
   c. Nobody saw submarines as having any useful purpose before 1879.
   d. The crew needed to build up their muscles so they could propel the submarine faster.

8. **An antonym for 'impenetrable' is**
   a. watertight
   b. unbreakable
   c. porous
   d. lengthy

9. **9. Work on submarines has gone on**
   a. since the 1700's
   b. since 1879
   c. for more than 350 years
   d. since last century

10. **What is 'impossible to verify' in the second paragraph?**
    a. Whether the vessel was a submarine or a submersible.
    b. Whether the vessel was self-propelled.
    c. Whether the trial was successful.
    d. Whether the vessel submerged successfully.

11. **An antonym for 'impenetrable' could be**
    a. flimsy
    b. impassable
    c. substantial
    d. wide-ranging

12. **Which of these facts can be found in the text?**
    a. The Turtle was financed by a group of businessman.
    b. The Eagle was eventually sunk.
    c. The Dutchman, Cornelius Drebbel, was in the service of the British.
    d. Garnett's steam engine was relatively small.

13. **'Ultimately successful' means**
    a. satisfactory in each attempt
    b. finally satisfactory
    c. initially satisfactory
    d. randomly satisfactory

14. **The purpose of the text is**
    a. humorous
    b. persuasive
    c. querying
    d. informative

15. **This text might be found in**
    a. A scientific magazine.
    b. A picture book of submarines.
    c. A history of the ships.
    d. A collection of strange and bizarre facts.

Read the extract and answer the questions that follow.

In Medieval times, long before the discoveries of penicillin and of the necessity of antiseptics, many bizarre remedies were administered to unhappy patients. Most sick people were not treated by doctors or physicians who lived in the cities and catered only to the upper classes. Instead they might go to barber-surgeons, to monks or to folk healers. Barber-surgeons cut hair, pulled teeth and did common operations such as those for hernias or gallstones. The monks saw treating the sick as an act of mercy and monasteries always included an infirmary and a garden where medicinal herbs were cultivated. Folk healers were usually women and they also used herbal potions along with some other strange folk remedies.

To prevent illness, people often wore necklaces of angelica (wild celery). Garlic was thought to have a similar effect as well as being a 'cure-all'. In a vain attempt to avoid contracting the Plague, some people dosed themselves with copious amounts of a mixture of garlic and mustard.

Cooked apples were often given as a first treatment for any illness. If the fever did not abate, the patient was given a spider wrapped in a raisin. Children who were ill were passed three times through a hoop made of dried honeysuckle.

In those times, it was believed that touching the tooth of a dead man would cure a toothache. Goose droppings were rubbed into the heads of hopeful men as a cure for baldness. Basil was mixed with powdered vulture's beak to heal tumours. Nettles whisked with white of egg were prescribed as a remedy for insomnia (difficulty in sleeping).

1. **"The heads of hopeful men" is an example of**
   a. exaggeration
   b. onomatopoeia
   c. alliteration
   d. metaphor

2. **Who would perform a small operation in Medieval times?**
   a. a doctor
   b. a folk healer
   c. a barber-surgeon
   d. a monk

3. **For what were goose droppings a cure?**
   a. hernia
   b. plague
   c. insomnia
   d. baldness

4. **What was the treatment for tumours?**
   a. nettles whisked with white of vulture's egg
   b. garlic mixed with mustard
   c. basil and powdered vulture's beak
   d. hoops of dried hyacinth

5. **Which words tell us that the preventative for the Plague was ineffective?**
   a. a vain attempt
   b. to avoid contracting
   c. in copious amounts
   d. a mixture of garlic and mustard

6. **What is the best meaning for 'cure-all'?**
   a. medication
   b. universal remedy
   c. potion
   d. preventative

7. **Which one of these statements is correct?**
   a. Garlic was used to treat fever.
   b. Angelica was used to treat toothache.
   c. Wild celery was useful in reducing fever.
   d. Monks used herbal remedies to help the sick.

8. **Which of these words is an antonym for 'abate'?**
   a. terminate
   b. oscillate
   c. escalate
   d. levitate

9. **Which fact cannot be found in the text?**
   a. The majority of folk healers were women.
   b. Barber-surgeons were lower class.
   c. Sleep problems are called insomnia.
   d. Penicillin did not exist in Medieval times.

10. **The purpose of this text is**
    a. to persuade and caution
    b. to inform and warn
    c. to instruct and amuse
    d. to inform and entertain

11. **What do you think 'infirmaries' might be?**
    a. large halls
    b. small hospitals
    c. dormitories
    d. dining rooms

12. **Why might monasteries have had infirmaries?**
    a. Barber-surgeons would not treat everyone.
    b. The monks wished to extend help to the sick.
    c. The monks wanted to make use of their home-grown herbs.
    d. People did not like the strange remedies provided by faith healers.

13. **A synonym for 'copious' could be**
    a. minute
    b. regular
    c. constant
    d. profuse

14. **Which statement could summarise the entire text?**
    a. People were much healthier in the Middle Ages.
    b. Folk remedies were surprisingly successful.
    c. The 'cure' was sometimes worse than the illness.
    d. We could try some of these bizarre cures today.

15. **Which book might this text form part of?**
    a. Ancient Remedies for Modern Patients.
    b. Medieval Myths
    c. A Handbook of Herbal Medicine.
    d. Life in the Middle Ages.

Read the extract and answer the questions that follow.

Have you ever wondered how tunnels are built under water? It is not possible to use the explosive techniques employed with tunnels through rock. There were many unsuccessful attempts and it seemed that underwater tunnels were just a far-fetched notion until the brilliant engineer Marc Isambard Brunel came on the scene. In 1818, he devised a cast-iron and wood

tunneling shield. This massive cylinder allowed thirty-six men to work within it while more workers followed behind to line the tunnel with bricks. The key innovation in this technique was the way the cylinder supported the unlined soft ground around and in front of it. In other tunneling attempts underwater this had collapsed, frequently with fatal results.

Brunel began, in 1825, to build the first tunnel beneath the Thames River in London. The process was not without problems. The tunnel flooded on several occasions. Methane gas seeped in from the sewage laden river above, causing the risk of fire and explosions, as well as making Brunel and his men very ill. Finance was a constant problem and at one time, as a clever money-making scheme, people were allowed to view the work in progress for a fee of a penny apiece.

The Thames tunnel was eventually finished in 1843. It was 408 metres in length, eleven metres wide and six metres high. Sadly, it was never used in the manner Brunel intended as a roadway for horse-drawn vehicles and soon became the haunt of small stall-holders and petty thieves. Ultimately, the tunnel became part of the Underground train system. In more recent years, it has been strengthened by encasing it in concrete and is still in use as a train tunnel.

There are many underwater tunnels in the world today, much longer and constructed using more elaborate techniques, but that does not diminish Brunel's amazing achievement.

1. A 'far-fetched notion' would be
   a. a feasible concept
   b. an attractive idea
   c. a fanciful thought
   d. a really good plan

2. "At last, Brunel's tunnel was fulfilling the vital purpose for which it had been designed: transporting people and goods under the Thames." To which paragraph should this be added?
   a. first
   b. second
   c. third
   d. fourth

3. **Why did earlier attempts to tunnel underwater fail?**
    a. There were many fatalities.
    b. The soft earth was not propped up with anything.
    c. Explosives designed for rock were used.
    d. Not enough men could work at one time.

4. **Which of these statements is true?**
    a. Many businessmen were keen to fund the tunnel.
    b. The tunnel has remained unchanged since completion.
    c. Stalls were set up to raise finance for the tunnel.
    d. Methane gas was an ever present danger.

5. **The text suggests that Brunel was**
    a. an impractical dreamer
    b. a creative thinker
    c. a kind benefactor
    d. a lazy genius

6. **Which of these statements best expresses the ideas in the last paragraph?**
    a. Although Brunel's tunnel represented a break-through, many more sophisticated tunnels have been built since then.
    b. Brunel's tunnel was good for his time, but it doesn't compare with modern tunnels.
    c. Even though since Brunel's time many longer tunnels have been built, his tunnel was a revolutionary achievement.
    d. Brunel's tunnel will eventually seem insignificant as longer tunnels are built.

7. **A synonym for 'key innovation' is**
    a. basic element
    b. essential improvement
    c. tried formula
    d. proven result

8. **'Haunt' in the third paragraph is**
    a. a finite verb
    b. a participle
    c. a noun
    d. a gerund

9. **The writer's attitude towards Brunel is**
    a. judgemental
    b. disinterested
    c. belittling
    d. positive

10. **Which statement is true?**
    a. The tunnel fell out of use in 1825.
    b. The finished tunnel was eleven metres high.
    c. The tunnelling shield was encased in concrete.
    d. The tunnel was intended as a road for horse-drawn traffic.

11. **Which statement is false?**
    a. The tunnel was finished in 1843.
    b. The tunnel was 408 metres long.
    c. Work on the tunnel began in 1818.
    d. The tunnel is still being used.

12. **An antonym for 'ultimately' would be**
    a. finally
    b. initially
    c. consequently
    d. deliberately

Read the extract and answer the questions that follow.

Dragons feature in the myths of many countries: China, India, Japan and Vietnam. In the English legend, the heroic St George is reputed to have slain a mighty dragon after a fierce and protracted battle.

    Most of these myths originated in the mists of antiquity. Small figures of dragons have been discovered in 5000 year old Chinese tombs. As crocodiles also have a very long history (their ancestors co-existed with the dinosaurs), it is possible that encounters with river-dwelling crocodiles gave rise to the myth of the dragon.

    Dragons have been seen as both benevolent and malevolent. In Asian legends, the dragons were well-disposed towards humankind. In China, it was believed that they could exercise benign control over the rain, the rivers and the sea, and that they used this ability to benefit people. After death, they gently bore the souls of the deceased to Heaven.

    Korean legends saw dragons in a similar light. King Munma, the monarch, who unified the Korean peninsula under the Silla kingdom, requested that after his death, his ashes be scattered in the Eastern Sea. When this eventually happened, a miraculous event occurred. His ashes were transformed into a sea dragon, which stood guard against foreign invasion for centuries.

    In Western literature, dragons have commonly been portrayed in a negative light. Often they have been pictured as jealously guarding hoards of dragon treasure or imprisoned abducted damsels against all comers. Killing a dragon was seen as a great achievement for any aspiring knightly hero like St George.

1. **The best meaning for 'the mists of antiquity' is**
    a. a hundred years ago
    b. in the dim, distant past
    c. comparatively recently
    d. in the time of the dinosaurs

2. **A 'protracted battle' is**
    a. short-lived
    b. brutal
    c. extreme
    d. extended

3. **By using words such as 'well disposed', 'benign' and 'gently' the writer underlines the idea that**
    a. dragons were portrayed positively in early myths
    b. dragons are seen in an optimistic way in myths from every country
    c. dragons can be viewed as benevolent or malevolent
    d. the depiction of dragons in Asian literature was affirmative

4. **'Co-existed with dinosaurs' means**
   a. co-operated with the dinosaurs
   b. lived at the same time
   c. weren't bothered by the dinosaurs
   d. are now extinct

5. **In which ways did Asian dragons benefit people?**
   a. guarding treasure and looking after abducted girls
   b. protecting against invasion and regulating nature
   c. defending against crocodiles and other dangers
   d. battling knights and taking souls to Heaven

6. **The purpose of the fourth paragraph is**
   a. to add to the history of dragons
   b. to give another perspective on dragons
   c. to provide more evidence of their benevolence
   d. to reveal the magical powers of dragons

7. **The text suggests that the main reason knights engaged dragons in battle was**
   a. to acquire treasure
   b. to rescue damsels in distress
   c. to become a saint
   d. to receive acclaim

8. **Which of these statements can be inferred from the text?**
   a. There have been some stories of benevolent Western dragons.
   b. Dragons are always depicted in a negative light in the West.
   c. Dragon stories are still very popular.
   d. Many dragons were actually killed by knights.

9. 9. **'In a similar light' means**
   a. early in the morning
   b. in the same area
   c. from a comparable perspective
   d. as Western literature portrays them

10. **The meaning of 'bore' in the last sentence of the third paragraph is**
    a. drilled
    b. wearied
    c. carried
    d. suffered

11. **'Hoards' in the last paragraph is**
    a. a finite verb
    b. a non-finite verb
    c. a verbal noun
    d. a noun

12. **The aim of the text is**
    a. to give an overview of dragon myths
    b. to justify negative stories of dragons
    c. to show that dragons are always benevolent
    d. to reveal the inner nature of dragons

13. **This text might feature in which of these?**
    a. 'Medieval Myths.'
    b. 'Global Myths.'
    c. 'Modern Myths.'
    d. 'Asian Myths.'

Read the extract and answer the questions that follow.

In Korea, in years long past, there lived a famous general, Kim Yu-sin who had a very good friend, a poor hermit. The name of this hermit has long been forgotten, but his deeds have not.

General Kim's kinsman, Suchon, had been languishing with a malignant disease for some months. Kim asked the hermit to leave his home, high up on a mountainside and come to the aid of his cousin. At the same time, Suchon had also asked his friend, a rich monk named Inhyesa, renowned for his magical powers, to visit him. The monk arrived and swept into Suchon's room where the hermit was already seated on the floor. "Who are you? You are not a doctor. You look shifty, like a fox!"

The hermit agreed that he was not a doctor, but was willing to do his best to help Suchon in his hour of need.

At this, the monk commanded, "Step aside! I will show you how I communicate with the spirits!" And, as he began chanting, varicoloured clouds appeared in the bedroom and fragrant blossoms rained down on the patient's bed. The monk regarded the hermit with a scornful expression.

"Oh that is very good," said the hermit. "But, I have a little magic art myself." With that, he touched the monk in the middle of his forehead. Immediately, the monk was wrenched up into the air by an invisible force, flung around in a somersault and smashed back into the ground where his head stuck fast, his legs stretched up towards the ceiling.

Everyone rushed to the monk and attempted to free him, but their efforts were fruitless. The hermit quietly left the room and did not return. Finally, Suchon sent a messenger to respectfully beseech the hermit to reverse the magic spell. He came, said, "Downside, up!" and the monk was again flung in a somersault and settled back onto his trembling feet. Shaken and contrite, he left and this allowed the hermit to concentrate on healing Suchon, which he did.

---

1. **A phrase with a similar meaning to 'languishing' is**
    a. complaining a lot
    b. suffering a great deal
    c. getting weaker
    d. pretending to be sick

2. **'Shifty' means**
    a. open
    b. clever
    c. quick
    d. suspicious

3. **'Shifty, like a fox' is**
    a. a metaphor
    b. personification
    c. modal language
    d. a simile

4. **Inhyesa's behaviour on first meeting the hermit is not**
    a. cautious
    b. arrogant
    c. hasty
    d. foolish

5. **Why did Inhyesa regard the hermit 'with a scornful expression'?**
    a. He was quite sure the hermit would try to help Suchon.
    b. He thought the hermit would be intimidated by his display.
    c. As a rich monk, he felt superior to a poor hermit.
    d. He expected the hermit to applaud the display.

6. **'At this, the monk commanded...' What does 'this' refer to?**
    a. The hermit's agreement that he had no medical qualifications.
    b. The monk's desire to dazzle everyone with his magic.
    c. The hermit's intention, despite the monk's scorn, to still offer any help he could.
    d. The monk's aggressive words to the hermit.

7. **Which of these statements is false?**
    a. The monk was twice tumbled in a somersault.
    b. The hermit touched the monk in the middle of his forehead.
    c. The command, "Upside, down", reversed the spell.
    d. The hermit did not return until summoned.

8. **Which of these statements cannot be inferred from the text?**
    a. The hermit was quietly confident of his own powers.
    b. This story can be read as a warning against over-confidence.
    c. The monk gave up practising magic after this experience.
    d. The monk was possibly less arrogant after this encounter.

9. **Why was the monk 'shaken and contrite'?**
    a. The hermit had threatened to do worse things to him.
    b. He had learned a valuable lesson in humility.
    c. He had been told his services were not required.
    d. He thought Suchon would be angry with him.

10. **A 'malignant' disease is**
    a. contagious
    b. malicious
    c. long-lasting
    d. likely to cause death

11. **Which word could not be a synonym for 'scornful'?**
    a. contemptuous
    b. mocking
    c. disrespectful
    d. unenthusiastic

12. **The message of the text is**
    a. not to show off
    b. not to complain
    c. to keep trying
    d. to welcome strangers

⊛ ANSWERS

Unit 1: Rubber
1. c	2. b	3. b	4. b	5. d
6. b	7. c	8. d	9. d	10. a
11. 5, 6, 4, 2, 1 ,3			12. c	13. b
14. c	15. a	16. c	17. b	

Unit 2: Email from Emily
1. 6, 5, 3, 4, 1, 8, 7 and 2.

2. c	3. c	4. d	5. b	6. a
7. d	8. c	9. b	10. b	11. c
12. a	13. d	14. d	15. c	16. d

Unit 3: Coelacanths
1. b	2. d	3. b	4. d	5. b
6. c	7. c	8. b	9. b	10. c
11. c	12. d	13. b	14. d	15. b,f
16. a				

Unit 4: The Hanging Gardens
1. d	2. c	3. d	4. c	5. d
6. d	7. c	8. b	9. c	10. c
11. b	12. d	13. d	14. b	

Unit 5: The Legend of Icarus
1. c	2. b	3. c	4. d	5. a
6. c	7. d	8. d	9. a	10. b
11. d	12. d	13. a	14. d	15. b
16. c				

Unit 6: Going, going, gone.
1. b	2. d	3. b	4. c	5. b
6. c	7. d	8. d	9. d	10. b
11. d	12. c.	13. a	14. b	

Unit 7: Dog Tales
1. b	2. d	3. c	4. d	5. c
6. c	7. d	8. b	9. c	10. a
11. b	12. d	13. c	14. b	

Unit 8: Life in an Acorn
1. b	2. c	3. d	4. d	5. b
6. c	7. b	8. d	9. c	10. b
11. c	12. a	13. b		

Unit 9: A Close Shave
1. c	2. c	3. b	4. d	5. b
6. c	7. a	8. d	9. c	10. d
11. c	12. b	13. b	14. c	

Unit 10: Pearling
1. b	2. a	3. b	4. b	5. d
6. c	7. a	8. b	9. b	10. d
11. b	12. c	13. a		

Unit 11: The Eye of the Hurricane
1. b	2. c	3. b	4. b	5. c
6. d	7. c	8. b	9. d	10. c
11. a	12. d	13. b	14. d	

Unit 12: Tigers Threatened
1. c	2. a	3. d	4. c	5. b
6. b	7. b	8. a	9. b	10. c
11. b	12. c	13. d		

Unit 13: Monster Drool
1. c	2. d	3. c	4. b	5. d
6. b	7. c	8. d	9. b	10. d
11. d	12. c			

Unit 14: Rockets
1. b	2. d	3. c	4. c	5. c
6. b	7. d	8. c	9. a,c,f,g,h	
10. d	11. b	12. d	13. c	14. a
15. c	16. b	17. c	18. c	19. d

Unit 15: Slings
1. c	2. b	3. d	4. a	5. c
6. d	7. b	8. a	9.a,c,h,i	
10. d	11.b	12. d	13. b	14. b
15. a	16. c	17. b	18. b	19. d

Unit 16: Lichen

1. b	2. b	3. c	4. d	5. b
6. c	7. d	8. d	9. b	10. d
11. d	12. b	13. a	14. d	15. c
16. b				

Unit 17: Keeping Mice as Pets

1. c	2. d	3. c	4. b	5. c
6. c	7. d	8. b	9. a	10. d
11. b	12. c	13. d		

Unit 18: The Giant Octopus

1. c	2. c	3. c	4. b	5. c
6. a	7. b	8. b	9. c	10. b
11. a	12. d	13. c	14. d	

Unit 19: Life as a Cabin Boy

1. c	2. d	3. b	4. b	5. a
6. a	7. b	8. c	9. b	10. c
11. d	12. c	13. c	14. b	

Unit 20: The Snowy River Scheme

1. c	2. c	3. d	4. c	5. b
6. c	7. a, c, f		8. b	9. c
10. d	11. b	12. a	13. b	

Unit 21: Arthur – A Real Person?

1. d	2. b	3. c	4. b	5. b
6. c	7. d	8. d	9. c	10. d
11. b	12. c	13. b	14. d	15. a
16. b				

Unit 22: Gold

1. c	2. b	3. d	4. c	5. c
6. d	7. b	8. c	9. c	10. b
11. d	12. d	13. b	14. c	15. a

Unit 23: The Stolen Cat

1. c	2. b	3. c	4. c	5. b
6. b	7. c	8. d	9. b	10. d
11. a	12. d	13. b	14. b	15. b
16. d				

Unit 24: The Cockroach

1. b	2. c	3. a	4. d	5. d
6. b	7. b, e, h, i, j		8. c	9. b
10. b	11. d	12. c	13. d	14. b

Unit 25: Come to Dinner

1. c	2. b	3. b	4. d	5. b
6. d	7. b	8. b	9. d	10. d
11. c	12. b	13. b	14. d	15. d
16. a	17. b, e, g, h		18. c	

Unit 26: The Sun

1. b	2. c	3. c	4. d	5. b
6. c	7. d	8. b	9. d	10. c
11. d	12. b	13. b		

Unit 27: Letters to the Editor

1. d	2. b	3. c	4. b	5. c
6. d	7. d	8. d	9. b	10. c
11. b	12. d	13. c	14. d	

Unit 28: William Tell

1. b	2. c	3. d	4. b	5. d
6. c	7. a	8. d	9. b	10. c
11. d	12. b	13. b	14. c	15. a
16. d	17. b	18. d	19. b	20. d
21. c				

Unit 29: What is Diwali?

1. d	2. b	3. b	4. c	5. d
6. c	7. d	8. a, c, d, e, h	9. b	
10. b	11. d	12. b	13. c	14. a

1. d   2. b   3. c   4. b   5. d
6. b   7. d   8. c   9. b   10. b
11. c   12. d   13. b

Unit 31: Sauropods

1. b   2. d   3. c   4. c   5. d
6. c   7. c   8. d   9. b   10. d
11. b   12. c   13. d   14. a

Unit 32: The Tale of Paddy

1. b   2. b   3. d   4. c   5. d
6. a   7. d   8. b   9. d   10. c
11. b   12. d   13. d   14. a

Unit 33: The Book of Kells

1. c   2. b   3. c
4. a: T, b: T, c: F, d: T, e: F, f: F
g: T, h: T5. d   6. c   7. c   8. b
9. c   10. b   11. b   12. d

Unit 34: Cane Toads

1. b   2. c   3. d   4. c   5. b
6. d   7. b   8. d   9. b   10. d
11. b   12. d   13. c   14. d   15. b

Unit 35: Muhammad Ali

1. c   2. c   3. d   4. c   5. c
6. b   7. b   8. c   9. d   10. b
11. b   12. c   13. b   14. c   15. b

Unit 36: Early Submarines

1. c   2. b   3. c   4. d   5. c
6. d   7. b   8. c   9. c   10. b
11. a   12. c   13. b   14. d   15. c

Unit 37: Strange Remedies

1. c   2. c   3. d   4. c   5. a
6. b   7. d   8. c   9. b   10. d
11. b   12. b   13. d   14. c   15. d

Unit 38: Underwater Tunnels

1. c   2. c   3. b   4. d   5. b
6. c   7. b   8. c   9. d   10. d
11. c   12. b

Unit 39: Dragons

1. b   2. d   3. d   4. b   5. b
6. c   7. d   8. d   9. c   10. c
11. d   12. a   13. b

Unit 40: The Humble Hermit

1. c   2. d   3. d   4. a   5. b
6. c   7. c   8. c   9. b   10. d
11. d   12. a

Vocabulary Notes